GW01184671

POCKET GUIDES

TO THE PRIMARY CURRICULUM

Materials and their properties

Neil Burton

Provides the knowledge you need
to teach the primary curriculum

Author
Neil Burton

Editor
Dodi Beardshaw

Assistant Editors
Jeff Nosbaum
Dulcie Booth

Cover design
Joy Monkhouse
Rachel Warner

Designer
Mark Udall

Illustrations
Andy Miles
Garry Davies

Cover photograph
Calvin Hewitt

Published by Scholastic Ltd,
Villiers House,
Clarendon Avenue,
Leamington Spa,
Warwickshire CV32 5PR

Text © 2001 Neil Burton
© 2001 Scholastic Ltd

1 2 3 4 5 6 7 8 9 0   1 2 3 4 5 6 7 8 9 0

British Library Cataloguing-in-
Publication Data
A catalogue record for this book is
available from the British Library.

ISBN 0439-01756-4

CONTENTS

Materials and their properties
INTRODUCTION

What is a primary scientist?

There is an important distinction to be made between scientists and primary science teachers. A scientist follows a particular strand of science as far as possible in order to explain it. A primary science teacher tries to understand the scientific links between things around him or her, and to help others achieve a better understanding of them. A good primary science teacher is interested in helping children to understand ideas, explain them and link them together. The words 'explore', 'investigate' and 'Why do you think that happened?' are much more likely to come from such a teacher than 'Learn this by heart' or 'You don't need to understand it, just remember it!'

How can this book help?

Having taught primary science within primary schools, initial teacher education and continuing professional development over the last fifteen years, I am convinced that there has been a steady improvement in the level of teachers' background science knowledge. I am less convinced that this has been entirely transferred to an understanding of the concepts at a level at which teachers are secure and confident. To have a level of understanding that allows you to pass on 'facts' with a fair degree of accuracy is not enough. You need to have a 'feel' for the subject that will allow you to appreciate where the children are 'coming from' and enable you to help them learn more effectively.

This book attempts to avoid a 'GCSE science – revisited' approach. GCSE textbooks serve a particular purpose well: to get pupils through a particular type of science exam. Primary school teachers have a very different need: to develop a clear and focused understanding of the science in order to be able to teach it effectively to others.

The idea of 'keeping one page ahead in the book' is now, surely, long gone. Teaching is much more than the passing on of facts for future regurgitation by a new generation of learners. Before teaching comes assessment and planning. Initial assessment is needed to reveal the children's ideas, to find out what they know and what they don't. Once you move on to finding out what their level of understanding is, things start to become less clear, but this is necessary in order to find out where the learning should start. After assessment comes planning: deciding on the ideas that you want the children to develop and the challenges, tasks and questions that you expect will get them there. Finally, there is the delivery: the teaching and learning that will see the plans come to fruition. Such a process can be embedded in the science curriculum for a key stage, or can be part of a pupil/teacher interaction lasting a few seconds. The key is understanding where the children are, where they need to go next and how to get them there – that is, understanding the science.

This book does not try to give you all the scientific facts you will ever need as a teacher. That's impossible: science is changing far too quickly. What it will attempt to do, largely through clear explanations, models and analogies, is to help you to reach a better understanding of the science – to help you visualise what is happening. Some of the science has been simplified in an attempt to clarify the ideas, but every effort has been made to ensure that the material is scientifically correct.

Structure of this book

Each area of science is broken down into a few **key concepts**. These are the ideas used as a focus for the development of explanations and examples. Together they form the basis of the elements within each strand of science of which children (and consequently you) need to develop a secure understanding.

A **concept chain** is included to provide a clear indication of progression and development. The chain goes beyond Key Stage 2, in order to help you see where the children are going. Scientific understanding is a never-ending quest; but an appreciation of where a child is in the learning continuum allows previous points to be reinforced and the next ones to be explored. With any scheme of work, a sense of place and direction is essential for all concerned.

The **subject facts** provided have three main purposes:
● To help you understand the ideas so that you can teach them effectively. (The explanations will often go beyond what you need to teach at Key Stage 2.)
● To show where the children will be going next with their learning.
● To make it easier for you to identify where the children have developed misconceptions.
Connected to this is a list of the important technical **vocabulary** that will be required to teach and understand these key ideas. It is especially important for the children to realize that some words used in general conversation have particular and explicit meanings in science, and to begin to appreciate when they need to apply this scientific usage.

Children are generally fascinated by **amazing facts**. Each scientific theme includes a few with which you can impress the class. They are mostly chosen to give some idea of the scale or extremes within the topic.

An understanding of some **common misconceptions** and what you might do about them is important in both assessment and planning. If you are aware of ways in which children might hold misconceptions, you can plan activities in such a way that children holding these ideas can be identified. Focused teaching can then be effectively employed. This section offers advice on identifying and rectifying pupil misconceptions.

Some common **questions** that children frequently ask about the phenomena and processes within particular areas of science are presented, together with suggestions on how they can be answered to give children an understanding of the science involved. However, the answers may not always provide a full explanation!

Further ideas for practical **teaching activities** are provided, with a focus on particular approaches (exploring, investigating, sorting and classifying) and on the use of ICT to enhance learning. Where possible, specialist science equipment is avoided. This helps to link the science to familiar and practical contexts. However, in some cases particular equipment is necessary for measuring or collecting, or is required for health and safety reasons. The ICT activities depend on a certain level of hardware and software availability: word and data processing facilities; the ability to capture sound and images and incorporate them into presentation software; remote data capture (for example, temperature probes). The use of the Internet should be encouraged, but reference to it is restricted here because of the transitory nature of many websites.

Approach to teaching and learning

This book leans towards a particular learning theory – without, I hope, slavishly following it. The constructivist approach to the teaching of science has developed over many years and is now acknowledged as a highly effective way of ensuring that children develop scientific abilities on the basis of a secure foundation in scientific concepts. Constructivism attempts to avoid teaching children an understanding of a scientific process or phenomenon while, at the same time, allowing them to continue to hold a conflicting conception. It is easy for a child to believe two very different explanations for the same concept concurrently. They may have been told one explanation at school and use it to respond when the teacher asks, but hold another, arising from their empirical observations, which they use the rest of the time (for example, 'Plants go to sleep at night').

To adopt a constructivist approach, the teacher must first determine the area of science within which the children will need to work (from the curriculum or the school's scheme of work). This will help the teacher to identify the range of ideas and misconceptions that the children might hold. Next, the teacher needs to identify a stimulus or context that will help the children to focus on the topic by engaging their interest in something familiar. The next three stages depend on the children. In the first stage, the stimulus or context is used to elicit the children's ideas, with the teacher questioning and probing to discover the extent of their understanding. Based on this assessment, the teacher plans a range of highly focused activities, building on the children's questions and suggestions to reinforce correct ideas and challenge misconceptions. In a final assessment and reflection stage, the children are asked to consider how their understanding has changed. The teacher acknowledges progression and identifies the next steps to be taken.

This approach is about constructing a secure understanding of science based on broad and firm foundations, rather than requiring the children to retain transitory knowledge which they are unable to link to any pre-held ideas. However, there is a downside. This approach tends to take longer, both in the meeting of individual learning objectives and in terms of the coverage of content, than a more piecemeal approach. Although 'finding out where the children are starting from' is an essential prerequisite, it could mean that the teacher is attempting to help the children progress from many

different starting points. Applying probing questions to a whole class cannot be done both accurately and quickly – though if you have found a way, please get in touch! The recording of assessments is also very time-consuming, although it can be very satisfying to look back and register the progression. The teacher will need to group children with similar ideas and find an efficient way of charting misconceptions and progress.

Not only is constructivism a highly effective way of teaching children, it also encourages a reflective and professional approach from the teacher. It leads the teacher to examine and analyse every step of the teaching; this will aid the development of a better understanding of the individual children and their learning, as well as of the scientific ideas and the means of communicating them.

This book is dedicated to Martine, William and James, who have continually asked me 'why' during the writing of this book – admittedly, mostly in the context of asking 'Why haven't you finished writing that book yet, Dad?'

Chapter 1
THE NATURE OF STUFF

Key Concepts

The ideas contained in the primary curriculum concerning the nature of materials only begin to appear formally during Key Stage 2, but even then they are at the descriptive rather than explanatory stage. Although the particular nature of matter does not appear until Level 6, children need to be prepared for this 'revelation' at an earlier age to avoid any potential conflict of ideas. It is also, possibly, the area of science where the teacher's understanding is expected to be most in advance of the pupil's. The key ideas to be developed here are that:

1. Materials can be described and defined in different ways.
2. Materials are made up of very small particles.
3. Molecular models can be used to describe and explain how arranging these particles in different, well-defined ways can make different materials.

The nature of 'stuff' concept chain

It is important to be aware of how these concepts might be developed. Below you can follow ONE way in which this progression can be traced. It includes Key Stage 3 because it is necessary to know what the children will be studying next. A useful way of demonstrating your own understanding of the concepts is to produce your own concept chain.

KS1

● All senses can be used to explore the physical properties of materials.
● Knowledge about the properties, names and sources of materials are important factors in their classification.

KS2

● Physical properties – such as states of matter – may vary with temperature.
● Different substances can be combined in mixtures.
● Some materials are found naturally, while others are manufactured.

KS3

● All materials are made from small particles called atoms.
● Some materials are made from only one type of **atom** (**elements**), while others are made of different types (**compounds**).
● Different materials, with different properties, can be made by combining atoms in different ways.
● Particle models of materials can be used to explain their physical properties.

Concept 1: Describing and defining materials

Subject facts

Defining 'materials'

All matter, that is everything around us – objects, animals, plants, the ground, the air – is made from materials. There are many, many different types of materials – and many of those are in a constant state of change, either changing from one type of material to another, or changing their state (between solid, liquid and gas). Plants turn a gas (the carbon dioxide in air) and water into solid vegetation, which animals then eat to become bigger before dying and decaying, releasing the carbon back into the environment once more. The nature of materials is like a construction kit – the same small pieces can be rearranged to construct many different objects.

Look around you. Consider the different objects you can see and the different materials from which they are made. It is important to separate objects from materials: an object may be made of several distinctly different materials, while one material may be used to make several distinctly different objects. In the same way that children learn to define what, for example, a 'chair' is, and how it is distinct from a 'table', through continuous and increasingly precise use of the terms, they can begin to sub-categorise chairs into different types (stools, sofas, thrones ...) by repeated usage. In a similar way, knowledge of materials can become increasingly more precise. We define all that is around us by agreeing the set of characteristics that distinguishes, for example, a 'metal' from a 'wood'. It is sometimes possible to confuse the issue when either imprecise or conflicting definitions are given or there is a confusion between object and material. We must always be precise that when we are talking about 'material', we are focusing on what it has been made from, not what it has been made into.

Describing materials

There are several groups of adjectives that are commonly used to describe materials, depending upon the senses or tests being used. These terms might relate to the texture, strength or optical qualities or one of a number of testable characteristics such as electrical conductivity. A material is recognised by the collection of known characteristics that it possesses.

If we examine the material 'glass', for example, we must start by focusing on the material rather than an object of the same name. A 'glass', though often made of glass, is often the name given to a drinking vessel without a handle (though sometimes 'beaker' is used). 'Glasses', that is, spectacles, frequently have no glass content at all, especially since hardened plastic lenses are safer to wear. So the objects that have been given their name by the original material, now may not contain the material at all. So what characteristics spring to mind when you think of the material 'glass'? Transparent, brittle, hard ...?

Polystyrene is a clear plastic that is often used as an alternative to glass (particularly for drinking vessels). (As an aside, if you are wondering about those 'polystyrene' cups from hot drink vending machines or the packaging material – this is *expanded* polystyrene: rigid foam made of polystyrene and air.)

How can you distinguish between polystyrene and glass? Well, glass is denser – of two identical 'glasses' the plastic one will be lighter. Glass shatters more readily than the plastic but is more resistant to scratching – hardly constructive though is it? Neither is it particularly helpful to test by seeing which one melts first when exposed to high temperatures (it's the plastic). Try tapping both materials with something hard, a coin or even a finger nail – the glass will give a much clearer, sharper sound than the polystyrene. Why? – because of the structure of the material (and that's what most of this book is about, so read on).

Materials are also frequently described in terms of where they came from, particularly whether they were found naturally or whether they have been manufactured – for example in clothing to indicate the source of the fibres (and often the proportions in which they have been used).

Object and material

It is often quite easy to confuse the property of the material with the property of the object into which it has been made. A material may be dense, but an object would be described as heavy (in terms of mass). The distinction between the object and the material must be highlighted at each stage of work with the children. When comparing materials, the 'object' issue can be avoided to a very large extent if standard samples (size and shape) are used. Frequently objects are made from a combination of more than one material, to make the best use of the individual characteristics of each – this can also cause confusion when testing or observing objects in place of materials. Material samples need to be uniform.

These points will be covered in more detail in Chapter 2.

Why you need to know these facts 	The word 'material' has many different meanings, which are determined by context. An understanding of this key terminology and the different types of material is fundamental to further work in this area of science.
Vocabulary 	**Atom** – the smallest 'lump' of an element. **Compound** – a material made from different atoms chemically blended together in precisely the same proportions throughout. **Element** – a material made from only one type of atom.
Common misconceptions 	*Material is fabric.* This is another example of the problems caused by the imprecise use of English in common usage. To rectify the misunderstanding, children need to be reminded that particular words have a more specific meaning when they are used in the context of science (just like 'animal').

Why can't you use words like 'heavy' to describe a material?

Because words like 'heavy', 'big' or 'bendy' depend more upon the size and shape of the piece of the material than the material itself. A large block of glass, for example, would be big, heavy and rigid but fibre optics (the same material) would be small, light and bendy.

Word lists (research, recording)

In groups or as a class, the children can produce lists of adjectives to be used to describe materials and objects. Discussions will need to take place to decide if the words relate more appropriately to materials or objects that can be made from different materials.

Concept 2: Particles

Small bits

In about 400BC, the Greek philosopher Democritus coined the term 'atom' to describe the smallest possible 'lump' of any material that you could possibly get. For any one, pure type of material, or element, each of these atoms will be identical. Unfortunately this idea did not really catch on in western European science, and over the next 2000 years scientists thought along the lines that all matter contained four elements in different proportions. This may not seem too bad, until you realise that the elements they were talking about were 'air', 'fire', 'water' and 'earth'. Wood, for example, was deemed to be made of earth (the hard stuff) and water (the sap); when it was burnt it released the fire within and also the air (smoke) – well, it all seemed very convincing at the time!

It wasn't until 1807 that the English scientist, Dalton, was able to make any advance on the Greek atom theory. For materials that are made up of a consistent mix of different atoms (such as water: two parts hydrogen for one part oxygen) the smallest part is called a compound molecule. It will always be made up of whole numbers of atoms (so you can't get a small piece of water made from a hydrogen atom and half an oxygen atom!). This was a huge step forward and led directly to the development of a list of known chemical elements based upon their relative masses by Mendeleev in 1869 (the basis of the periodic table). It was even possible for chemists to start looking for new chemicals with particular theoretical properties based upon gaps in the list.

At the beginning of the twentieth century, Rutherford and Bohr realised that atoms were made from still smaller particles. These smaller 'sub-atomic' particles determined what the atom was going to be. While Rutherford described the atom as a **nucleus** sitting at the centre of a cloud of **electrons**, Bohr's version was a little more structured. Bohr

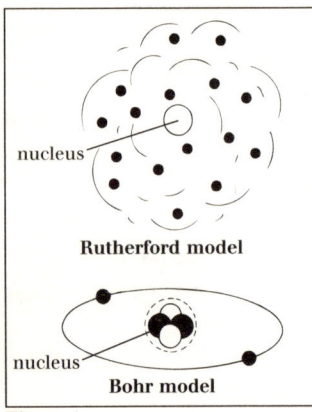

nucleus

Rutherford model

nucleus

Bohr model

Figure 1

visualised the atom as being like a mini solar system (see Figure 1), except that there were only certain 'orbits' that were possible. At the centre of the atom, the nucleus, lie the larger, more massive particles: **protons** (which have a positive charge) and **neutrons** (which have no charge). Outside of the nucleus the atom will have the same number of electrons (much less massive, negatively charged particles) as there are protons in the nucleus. Since then there have been a number of further advances to atomic theory with the

discovery of ever smaller particles with names like quarks, muons and mesons. But it doesn't end there. Quarks, for example, are described as coming in different 'flavours' (six to be precise: up, down, top, bottom, charm and strange), each of which can be in three different types or 'colours' (red, blue and green – though they have absolutely nothing to do with actual colours). It would seem that we have reached a point in science where all the sensible names have been used up! These sub-sub-atomic particles are themselves thought to be constructed from a fundamental particle, nicknamed 'string'.

There are certain 'general rules' that most atoms seem to obey.

1. There will be the same number of electrons and protons – otherwise the atom will either have an overall negative (too many electrons) or positive (not enough electrons) charge (these are called **ions**).

2. There are the same (or very nearly the same) number of neutrons as protons in the nucleus of an atom.

3. Only so many electrons can 'orbit' the nucleus at each level (or 'shell'). These shells, which fill up from closest to the nucleus, can contain a maximum of two electrons in the first shell and eight electrons in subsequent ones.

Asking children to use their imaginations within science is no bad thing. The development of models and theories later in their scientific development is based on this openness to new ideas that cannot be directly observed.

Electron – a small (in sub-atom sized terms) negatively charged particle.
Ion – an atom that has either gained or lost an electron to give it a negative or positive charge.
Neutron – a relatively massive (in sub-atom sized terms) neutrally charged particle.
Nucleus – the centre of the atom containing protons and neutrons.
Proton – a relatively massive (in sub-atom sized terms) positively charged particle.

● The biggest naturally occurring atom (uranium 238) is 0.000 001mm across and weighs 0. 000 000 000 000 000 004g – proportionally there is the same difference between this atom and 1g as there is between 1g and the mass of the Earth!
● Uranium 238 is called that because it weighs 238 times as much as an atom of hydrogen – the smallest possible atom (just one proton and one electron).

Atoms are like little solar systems.
Although it is sometimes convenient to visualise models of atoms in this way, they certainly are nothing like little solar systems. It is important to distinguish between models and reality. Models are there purely to help explain certain characteristics by linking to something with which the individual may have more experience or familiarity. A solar system is based upon spheres of different sizes moving in different orbits around a central star. This model offers a central point (nucleus) made from a number of two different types of particle, surrounded by a number of electrons (all of the same mass) held at particular energy levels, which the model chooses to present as orbits at a particular distance from the nucleus. The solar system analogy gets you thinking along the right lines initially to follow the model, but it quickly moves off on a different track.

Questions

Am I (the teacher) expected to teach this to primary school children?

No – well at least not yet! It is included here because this understanding of the atom is part of the necessary scientific knowledge that all primary teachers are expected to possess.

Concept 3: Molecular models

Subject facts

Chemistry is basically a construction kit

If you know how the bits (atoms mainly) fit together you can construct some pretty incredible things. In building with atoms, the main thing to remember is that atoms have an 'urge' to join up with other atoms in order to 'complete' or fill the outermost of their electron shells. If the outermost electron shell is already full then the atom will be quite happy to remain on its own. In fact it will be particularly difficult to make such atoms join up with any others. There are a few unusual atoms like this that don't react or combine with other atoms – as a group they are known as 'inert gases'. All other atoms have to be joined in groups of atoms for them to be stable. The first three inert gases, in terms of the number of electrons, are:

● Helium – two electrons (see Figure 1) which complete the first and only shell
● Neon – ten electrons (two in the first shell and eight in the next)
● Argon – 18 electrons (two in the first then eight in each of the next two shells).

The rules about how many electrons are required to complete a shell fall down after that, but the next three inert gases are trypton, xenon and radon – each having complete outer shells of eight electrons.

Joining atoms

There are two different ways that atoms can join together. The first is by 'sharing electrons', which is known as **covalent bonding**. The hydrogen atom cannot exist in a free state on its own – it must bond with another atom to complete its outer electron shell. By sharing electrons with another hydrogen atom (see Figure 2a), both now have two electrons in their outer shell. So two atoms of hydrogen joined in this way represent the smallest amount of the element hydrogen (the molecule H_2) you will ever find.

Oxygen has eight electrons (two in the first shell and six in the next – this is written like this: 2,6), so it needs two more electrons in the outermost shell to form a stable molecule. If it wants to join up with more oxygen, it can either share an electron with each of two other oxygen atoms (O_3) or provide two electrons in a bond with one other oxygen atom (forming a double bond, O_2). These are all still molecules that are elements, building with one type of atom at a time.

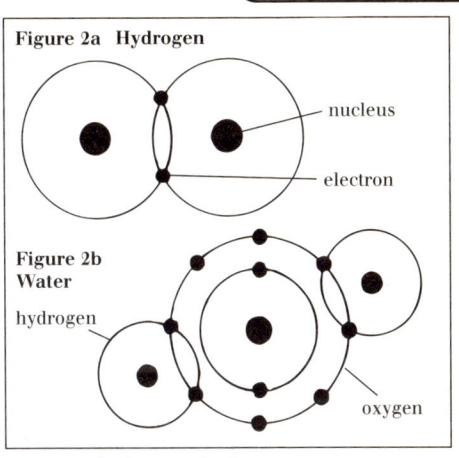

Figure 2a Hydrogen

nucleus

electron

Figure 2b
Water

hydrogen

oxygen

Atoms can be combined to form compounds in much the same way. Two atoms of hydrogen, each contributing an electron to the bond, can join with an atom of oxygen (Figure 2b) to form the compound 'water'.

Once you know how many electrons an atom has you can use these rules to bond atoms. Carbon (2,4) (see Figure 3a) is short of four electrons in its outermost shell. It can form two double bonds with two oxygen atoms to form carbon dioxide (CO_2). It can complete this outer shell by bonding with four hydrogen atoms to form a hydrocarbon called 'methane'. In fact it is possible to build a whole hydrocarbon family of large molecules by bonding carbon atoms together before attaching the hydrogen. Because carbon bonds so readily to other atoms (using single or double bonds) to form molecules, carbon can be found in 90% of the chemical compounds that occur naturally or are manufactured.

When atoms bond in this way, the molecules formed are relatively small and self-contained. Materials formed in this way tend to be gases and liquids at 'room temperatures'. It is possible to build incredibly long chains of hydrocarbons that are solids. If you add oxygen to your compound, you can form solid carbohydrates. These long carbon chains can have various other atoms attached to them to further change the properties of the compound. Building molecules such as these is the basis of materials such as plastics.

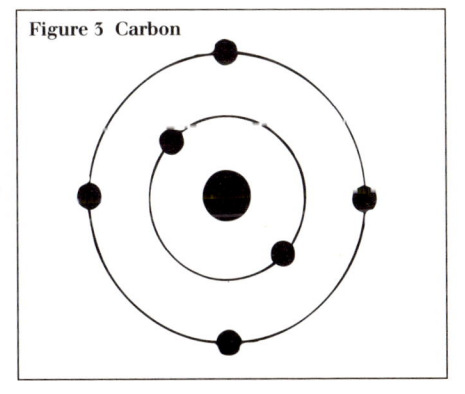

Figure 3 Carbon

Giant structures

If you want to build big atomic structures, really big ones that have the potential to go on and on, or at least until you run out of pieces, then ionic bonding is for you. This bonding relies on atoms losing and gaining electrons to complete their outermost shells. Some elements, such as sodium, with 11 electrons (2,8,1), have a single electron in their outer shell, whereas chlorine, with 17 (2,8,7), has only one 'gap' in its outer shell. When there are only a couple or so in an outer shell built for eight, they tend not to be well attached and are apt to 'wander off'. When sodium and chlorine are brought together, the rather loose sodium electron will wander off to fill the gap in the outer shell of the chlorine atom – thus forming a complete outer shell for both (see Figure 4a). The only problem now is that the chlorine atom has one more electron than it has protons, giving it an overall 'negative charge', and the sodium will be an overall 'positive'. Charged atoms are called 'ions' – so we now have positive ions of sodium and negative ions of chlorine. Opposite charges attract so these ions collect together in a latticework (see Figure 4b).

These sorts of crystal structures can go on growing as long as there are ions available to add to them – but they tend not to be that large, since their crystalline structure makes them brittle. All that's needed is a slight push and rather than lining up positive/negative throughout, positives find themselves next to each other, causing them to repel each other and the structure to break. That's why you can usually manage to get sodium chloride (common salt) out through those little holes in the shaker! It is also the reason why it dissolves so easily in water – all those small granules give it a very large surface area.

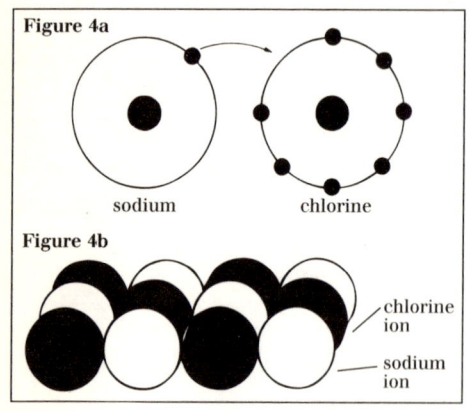

Figure 4a

sodium   chlorine

Figure 4b

chlorine ion

sodium ion

Glass is a very interesting material from a structural perspective – it is one of the hardest materials known and is very brittle, but, in fact, technically speaking it is neither really a solid nor a liquid! Although for practical purposes it is a solid, actually it is classed as a very viscous, extremely slow-flowing liquid. Its atomic structure is effectively a **giant structure**, made by the fusion of different types of silica (sand). This ionic structure makes it very strong but liable to shatter.

Metals

The collection of materials known as metals is a bit special – they are excellent conductors of heat and electricity, but what is it about their molecular structure that enables them to do this? All metals have one key characteristic in common – they only have, at most, a couple of electrons in their outermost shells. By having an incomplete outer shell, the one or two electrons in it (out of the complete set of eight), tend not to be very well attached to the atom. Sodium is a good example of a metal. Copper, silver and gold, all excellent conductors, only have one electron in their outer shells. Within a pure piece of metal, the electrons will flow randomly from atom to atom, allowing an excellent conductivity of heat. If a direct electric current is applied to a piece of metal, the electrons will be made to flow in a particular direction, so allowing electricity to be conducted. The bonding between the atoms of a metal also provide it with other useful characteristics, such as the ability to bend and keep a new shape. This is because the bonds between metal atoms are quite elastic. Initially a metal will bend and then return to its original shape as the molecular bonds snap back into position. If a metal is deformed too much, the bonds are broken and new ones form, holding the metal in a new position or shape.

Why you need to know these facts

Particle models are not required for children at KS1 and 2, but teachers need to be familiar and comfortable with them to ensure that what they teach will be consistent and compatible with the science that will follow. Particle models are a very good example of the use of the imagination in science to develop a way of visualising the unobservable.

Vocabulary

Covalent bonding – atoms held together through shared electrons.
Giant structure – an arrangement of ions of atoms, held together by attractive charges of positively and negatively charged ions (hence 'ionic' bonding).

Amazing facts

● In a diamond, each carbon atom is covalently bonded to four other carbon atoms. This crystalline structure is the hardest material yet found.
● Ethyne (CHCH) is a hydrocarbon with a triple covalent bond between the carbon atoms.

Common misconceptions

Diamond is made of pure carbon.
A diamond is certainly *mainly* made from carbon, particularly the internal structure, but that is not the complete story. In a diamond each carbon atom is connected to four other carbon atoms by single covalent bonds. This should mean that a diamond will continue to grow until all the carbon atoms are used up – but clearly diamonds are not *that* big! What happens at the surface of the diamond then? There must be carbon atoms that are short of an electron (one bond short) – which is not a state that can remain stable. To finish off all these 'loose ends', the final bond at the surface of a diamond is not with another carbon atom but with an atom of hydrogen – so when you touch a diamond you are actually touching hydrogen rather than carbon.

Questions

How real are the models?
The models are just that – models. They are useful in explaining reality, no more than that. They are not reality! The model provides a way of visualising atoms as pieces in a construction kit. There are over 150 pieces (atoms) in this construction kit, some of which are more durable than others, and there are many more of some pieces than others. So the materials that are made depend upon the atoms that are available and how you put them together.

Teaching ideas

Molecular modelling is not an aspect of chemistry that currently needs to be taught in the primary phase.

Resources

Collections of materials can be used as a stimulus for the above activity.

Posters of sub-atomic structure models may be displayed in the classroom, but it is not an aspect normally taught in the primary phase.

For your own use there are many excellent GCSE texts that will provide useful further information on atoms and molecular structure.

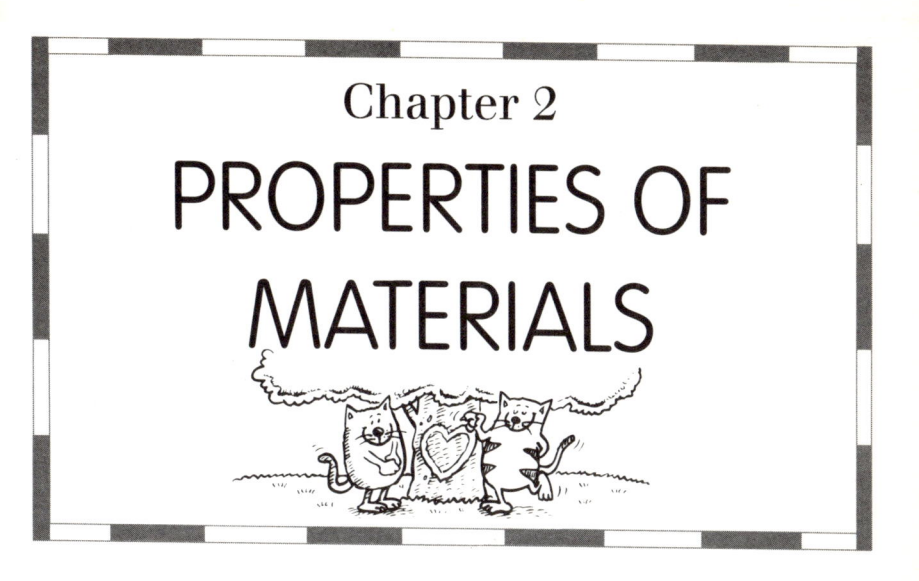

Chapter 2
PROPERTIES OF MATERIALS

The 'properties of materials' is a fundamental element of materials science at Key Stages 1 and 2. The ability to describe and later explain the properties of a given material is the basis of chemistry. By providing the children with a firm and secure grounding here, achievement can be more readily attained later. The key ideas to be developed here are that:

1. The properties of materials can be classified by their physical attributes.
2. These properties are determined by the structure of the material and these can be described using models.
3. Materials are often chosen because of their properties.

Properties of materials concept chain
See 'The nature of "stuff" concept chain' on page 12 for general comments.

KS1
● Similarities and differences between materials can be determined using various different senses.
● Materials can be classified and named according to their observable similarities and differences.
● Materials exhibit a variety of properties that allow them to be put to different uses.

● Specific materials are used for particular purposes on the basis of their properties.

KS2
● The properties of different materials can be compared by the application of simple tests.
● The uses of materials are determined by the properties they exhibit.
● Most physical properties are continuous rather than categoric variables.

KS3
● Most physical properties of materials can be explained using particular models.

Concept 1: Describing and defining materials

Subject facts

One of the things that humans always seem to be keen on doing – and children are little different in this respect – is giving things names. We ascribe names to living things and objects so that we can communicate successfully about them. If we ask a child to sit on a chair, they are unlikely to attempt to climb onto a cupboard ... Okay, perhaps that wasn't such a good example! They understand what 'chair' relates to in physical terms – they appreciate that chairs can look very different but they still contain that collection of characteristics that defines the object. They can accept subsets of 'chair' such as 'bench' or 'stool'. Children need to learn the rules by which we define things. The same is absolutely true of materials, but there are two key differences: firstly the terms and definitions are often not repeated sufficiently or in a sufficient number of contexts to 'take hold'; and secondly we ill-define them for children either through lack of opportunity or ignorance. Another problem is that scientists have a sneaky habit of trying to make some materials look like others! Can you be sure that it is really a *diamond* ring (and not glass or zirconium)?

We often build up a definition of a material through repeated examples without ever having to put that definition into words. What actually defines a piece of wood? What is the commonality between mahogany, oak and pine (and even balsa) that defines all of these as wood? Some types of particularly dense hardwood don't even float! Children have to deal with the difficulty of this lack of specific definition. Quite often our ability to identify materials (as in 'ah, that's plastic') is based upon our knowledge of the materials which are most often used to make particular objects. For example, if you were to observe that the chair on which you were about to sit had a raised and rounded seat with a colourful, shiny surface, your experience of such things might well tell you that you are about to sit on a plastic or possibly leather material that will be soft. So if it turned out to be carved and painted wood or metal you would be quite surprised by the unexpected hardness as you sat down.

When exploring the physical attributes of materials there are two basic approaches that can be taken:
1. examining the range of physical characteristics that a particular material possesses
2. examining a particular physical characteristic over a range of materials.
Either approach is valid, but as noted on page 13 it is important that the focus is on the material rather than on the object into which it has been made. For this reason it is always preferable to have uniform shapes and sizes of the materials to work with (material sets are available from educational suppliers).

The precise properties of solids, liquids and gases will be covered in Chapter 3 'Changing states'. In this chapter the focus will be exclusively on solid materials.

Object properties

Frequently it is difficult to differentiate between material and object properties. If you were to place a piece of a material in front of a group of children (or adults come to that), they would invariably begin to use terms that applied to the shape the material was in (that is, the object). It is all too easy to refer to properties of the object and ascribe them to the material. 'Steel is sharp' – well, it is if the object that it has been shaped into has a particularly acute edge to it. 'Granite is rough' – yes, but only because that particular piece has not been subject to the smoothing and polishing action of, for example, moving water. 'Plasticine floats' – but only when it is in a 'boat-like' shape. Some object properties might be more *technically* possible with some materials than others – for example, I would much more readily expect to find a cutting edge on an *object* made from a steel than Plasticine, but I would be hard pushed to cut myself on a steel ball-bearing!

For this reason, when attempting to define the properties of a material it is important to have a range of different examples of that material. Commonalties between those materials can then be established. What are the key factors (properties) that distinguish, say, steel from mahogany? The potential object properties, such as smoothness and sharpness, need to be disregarded in favour of those where the materials are distinctly different – in this case, electrical conductivity and magnetic effects.

Mechanical properties of materials

These properties can be described and explained also in terms of the structure of the material (see 'The structure of materials' on page 44). Such properties can either be revealed by simple handling of the materials, with the children using their own hands to test the characteristics, or through the use of fair tests where the relative merits of each material can be measured and compared numerically.

Hardness

This is a characteristic of the surface of a material. It relates to how readily the material is scratched or dented. Visual observation of this characteristic can only really be made as a result of a practical, tactile test. Both dents and scratches are the result of a force being applied over a given, usually relatively small, area. The greater the force required to make a mark, the **harder** the material is said to be. Simple tests performed by the children, such as poking the material with a finger or attempting to scratch it with a blunt point or edge of a known harder material (such as a large iron nail – appropriately supervised, of course), can give an indication of hardness. For rocks and minerals there is a special scale of 'hardness', the Moh scale (see page 113), ranging from 1 (talc – soft and crumbly) to 10 (diamond).

Fracture

Often this is where the object that the material has been made into can be brought more into focus than the actual material. Using identical samples of each material on which to perform tests can only accurately identify strong (or weak) materials. In practice children can quite easily draw the conclusion that the biggest piece of material is the strongest! (see Figure 1).

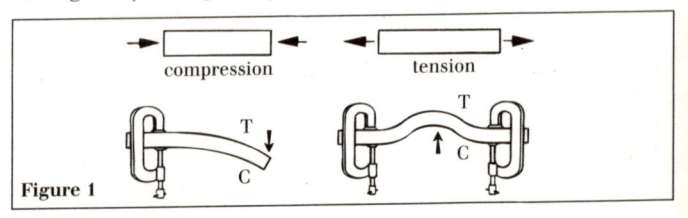

compression   tension

Figure 1

It is possible to measure the strength of an object by measuring the force required to break (fracture) it by means of compression, tension or bending. When you are focusing on the material, you are observing the way that it fractures. Does it break in one go (**brittle**)? Or does it 'give' and slowly fracture (**tough**)? It is possible that a material will be quite difficult to fracture because of its ability to change shape. Most brittle materials tend to give 'clean breaks' – either they are in one piece or several (try this for yourself with crockery!). Once the break has started, the material will be seriously weakened along this 'fault-line' and it is likely to take only a relatively minor force to 'finish it off'. A tough material, such as wood, may begin to break long before a more brittle material (in terms of the force applied) but will still be going through the breaking process long after the more brittle material has completed shattering. When a tough material completely breaks it is likely to be rough or splintered, a contrast to the brittle material. A tree in the wind, for example, will bend and flex, producing creaking sounds as it does so, but it will not necessarily break. In very strong winds, branches may even begin to splinter, but only with sustained and repeated bending backwards and forwards are they likely to break completely. A sheet of glass, such as a window, on the other hand, does not go through this gradual breaking process. To some extent glass will flex – surely everyone has experienced that gut-wrenching sensation of watching a ball bounce off next door's front window and that feeling of relief as the glass vibrates but stays in one piece! Unlike wood, there will be no signs of the glass having been weakened (just the tell-tale round splodge). When glass does break the fracture is complete and instantaneous. There are no fibres that break one at a time, simply a complete dislocation along a plane. Now you've got one piece of glass ... now you've got lots of pieces!

Deformation

When a force is applied to some materials they can be made to change shape without breaking. They are described by what happens when the force is removed – for example, you stop bending it. If the material returns to its original shape, it is known as **elastic**. If it remains in the shape into which it has been changed, it is defined as **plastic**. (Please note – not all *plastics* (the group of materials) are *plastic* (the mechanical property). Annoying isn't it!) Materials that can be deformed, such as rubber, can be both plastic and elastic – the first time that you stretch a new rubber band it will not return completely to its original length. The extent to which an object can be deformed is known as *stiffness* – if it is very difficult to deform it is known as *rigid*, and easy to deform, *flexible*. Plasticine (the name is a strong hint!) is an excellent example of a plastic modelling material.

Strength

Strength is quite a familiar property to consider – at least superficially! The property is also applied to objects as well as materials in the general sense of its use – newspaper would not normally be regarded as a strong material, but roll it up into a tight tube (an object) then it will be seen to be quite *strong* under compression. A strong material (or object) will be one that resists bending or fracture when a force is applied. Again it is vitally important that when comparisons are made they are done on a fair basis with forces being applied consistently in the same direction(s). When testing materials, they need to be of the same shape, and when testing the strength of objects, they need to be made from the same material. If, in a design and technology (as opposed to science) context, the strength of different designs is being tested (different objects and materials to serve the same purpose) it would be appropriate to keep some factor, such as some measure of 'cost', consistent between the designs in order to ensure an equivalent use of resources – products are often designed with a particular cost or price in mind. (The approach will be either to produce the highest quality product within the constraints of cost, or to meet as cheaply as possible a minimum quality threshold.) A strong elastic band will be one that requires considerable force to stretch it (change the shape), while a strong brick may be one that can withstand a considerable amount of pressure before crumbling (breaking under the force of compression).

Optical properties

The three main categories that refer to how light travels through materials are **transparent**, **translucent** and **opaque**. The distinctions between these three categories are rather blurred. While glass is clearly (sorry!) an excellent and frequently used example of a transparent material, if it were to be particularly thick, full of impurities or scratched on the surface, the transmission of images would be significantly reduced. Thickening the glass will result in more of the light being absorbed as it attempts to travel through. Even relatively thin sheets of glass absorb some light. If you observe the effects of light coming through the glass in a window and compare this to light coming through an open window (that is, no glass), you will see that the area lit by the light through the window will be in partial shadow. Hold a piece of glass between the Sun and a wall and you will see the shadow of your arm and hand and the partial shadow of the glass on the wall. Using thicker or frosted glass will make this shadow deeper still.

Certain impurities in the glass can be very particular about what light they allow to travel through. Adding metal oxides to glass as it is being made will allow the finished glass to transmit certain colours of light and absorb others. Adding iron oxide will allow red (but not blue or green) light to be transmitted through the glass; copper oxide will give a green filter and cobalt oxide gives a blue filter to the glass. The glass is still transparent so it is possible to see images through it, but it is only transparent for certain frequencies of light and is opaque for others.

Tracing paper is an interesting material as it is possible to see images through the paper if it is held close against an object, but it is not possible to see more distant objects. For this reason, materials such as tracing paper are defined as translucent rather than transparent. Similarly, fabric, such as single thickness curtains or your shirt, are opaque (for obvious reasons!), but if you bring your face very close to the fabric you will be able to see through it. This does not mean that your clothing can be described as transparent, only that in special circumstances sufficient light can get through the fabric to allow you to see. If the fabric is stretched out, it is possible to see objects where the light from them travels between the fibres of the fabric. The denser the fabric fibres are packed, the more opaque the fabric is – in effect you are not actually looking through the fabric, you are seeing the light that is travelling between the fibres of the fabric.

Translucency can be an internal property or depend on the surface of the material. A translucent material allows light to travel through but the light is scattered, making it impossible to view a clear image. Opaque particles within the otherwise transparent material may also alter the direction of the light, and may cause translucency. Alternatively, the path of the light may be altered as it enters or leaves the transparent material in a random way by scratches or other irregularities in the surface. The effect of a beach on a pair of plastic-lensed sunglasses is a good example of this – the surface of the lenses might get so scratched that you can't see through them, but this doesn't mean that the material they're made of is changed!

Optical properties on a surface

When light strikes the surface of a material it will either be scattered, reflected, absorbed or transmitted through transparent or translucent materials – or more likely, a combination of these. 'Reflections' refer to light being returned precisely in the form of images from the surface of an object; whereas 'scattering' refers to light being returned randomly.

Materials will often absorb some frequencies of light and scatter others, giving certain materials their particular colours. Copper oxide (this is copper when you haven't bothered to polish it for far too long, allowing it to react to the oxygen in the air or water) appears green – meaning that it absorbs red and blue frequencies of light and scatters green. Iron oxide (or 'rust') absorbs blue and green frequencies and scatters red. It is possible to change the surface colours of materials by covering them with paint – but then you are not actually looking at the material any more, are you?

Terms that are often used in describing the surface optics include 'dull', 'shiny', their reflectivity, colour, and consistency. It must be recognised that sometimes these will refer to the object that the material has been transformed into rather than the material itself – polishing can make many materials shiny, but it is easier to make some materials shiny than others (some are more naturally smooth). It is also possible that the material has been covered with something else, such as polish, which affects the optical qualities.

Density

The mass of a given volume of a material, *density*, is usually measured in either grams per cubic centimetre (gcm^{-3}) or kilograms per cubic metre (kgm^{-3}). It is usual to apply the gcm^{-3} approach, since $1cm^3$ (or millilitre) of water has a mass of 1 gram. What do gcm^{-3} and water have to do with it? Water has a density of $1gcm^{-3}$ and any material with a density above that will sink, and below that, will float. Apples, for example have a density slightly less than that of water, but pears are slightly more dense. This is why you go bobbing for apples (which float) rather than pears (which don't).

Every pure material has a specific density which can be compared to the density of water by attempting to float the material. Those that sink have a greater density and those that float are less dense. Clearly, the shape of the object that the material has been made into will be important – large steel objects (for example, ships) float because they enclose air. In an overall sense, taking the entire volume of the ship into account, they are less dense than water, allowing them to float. If you attempted to make a ship out of solid steel, or even replaced the air with water, it would become of a much greater density than water and so sink. On an atomic scale, heavier atoms, those with a greater number of sub-atomic particles (mainly neutrons and protons in the nucleus), form the denser materials.

Conductivity

There are two main forms of conductivity – electrical and heat-related. Conductors or conductive materials are ones that readily allow heat or electricity to flow through them. In general, those materials that are good electrical conductors are also good conductors of heat. This is one of the special properties of metals (see Figure 2).

As explained in 'Metals', on page 21, the electrons in a metal are only loosely attached to their nucleus, and are thus apt to 'wander around' randomly. In this model there are only a few electrons in the partially formed outermost shell. These electrons are the particles that 'flow' when a conductor is connected into an electrical circuit and a current is then applied. When these electrons flow they are, in effect, carrying energy through the material.

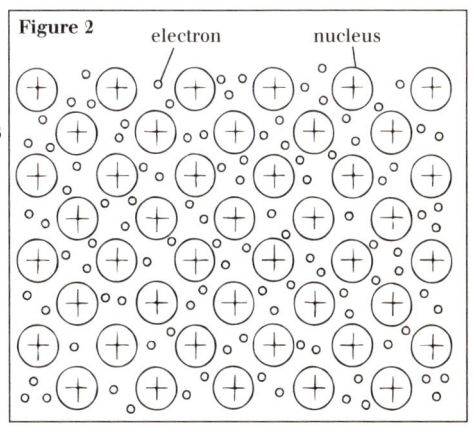

Figure 2   electron   nucleus

This energy can also be carried in the form of heat – which is, in effect, movement. When heat is applied to a conductive material it 'excites' the atoms – makes them begin to vibrate and take on more energy. This energy (vibrations) is transmitted from one atom to the next by the random movements of electrons. The more random movement of electrons there is, the faster the heat will be conducted through the material (and the better conductor it will be said to be).

Materials that are good thermal conductors will feel hotter (or colder) to the touch than poor conductors of the same temperature. Perhaps while doing the washing-up you will have noticed that metal utensils feel hotter than wooden or plastic ones that have been in the same bowl of hot water. This is not because they haven't all been heated to the same temperature, but because of how well they are able to transfer their heat energy to your hand. They will continue to transfer heat to your hand until they have cooled down to the same temperature that your hand has heated up to. A material that is a good conductor will allow this flow to happen much more quickly, making the material feel much hotter.

The same is true for a lack of heat (often known in the trade as 'cold'). If you have a few baked beans left over after your meal, you might well put them in the fridge to finish off the next day. If you leave them in the bare metal tin (without the paper label) the container will feel colder than if you leave them in a plastic container. As you retrieve the tin from the fridge, the heat in your hand will flow quickly into it since metal is a good thermal conductor.

The heat would flow slowly into the plastic pot, as it is a pretty good thermal insulator. Initially the plastic pot may feel a little cool, but this won't last long as the heat will not flow very far from where your hand is making contact. If you look carefully around the kitchen at the cooking utensils you should be able to make out which materials are good conductors of heat and which ones are not – in short, always be wary of metal-handled saucepans!

Poor thermal conductors are all around us – for example, in clothing. The fabric itself is a poor conductor of heat, but it adds to the insulation qualities by trapping air. Air is a particularly poor thermal conductor, especially if it is not allowed to flow. Your body warms a layer of air immediately surrounding your body which is trapped there by a layer of fabric and this is what keeps you warm – the greater number of layers, the warmer you will be. As strange as it may seem, not wearing any clothes may not necessarily make you any cooler – you will need to avoid any direct radiating sources of heat (the Sun for example) and arrange a flow of air over your body. This actually suggests wearing loose clothing of a colour that reflects the Sun's energy rather than absorbing it (the colour is important: generally the darker the colour the more that it absorbs light energy – see *Pocket Guides: Physical Processes*, page 101).

Electricity is the flow of electrons in a particular direction in a conductive material when that material is connected into a complete circuit (a concept that is explained in much greater detail in *Physical Processes*). The atomic structure of metal (see Figure 2) not only allows the flow of heat, but because the electrons are negatively charged particles, this also allows an electrical current to flow without offering too much resistance. Other materials offer much more resistance to the flow though none can really be called a complete 'non-conductor'. On a simple battery/bulb/wire circuit, it is necessary to have the circuit completed for the bulb to light. Holding a wire away from a terminal of the battery is enough to prevent the flow. This is because there is insufficient energy in the battery to force a way through the poor conductivity of the air. Even placing the two terminals in the same glass of water doesn't make matters any better.

A larger energy source (but for goodness sake and safety's sake DON'T try it!) such as mains electricity, would enable the electricity to force a way through the water only too well – it would even be able to 'jump' small air gaps, blasting the air molecules apart in a spark as it did so. Using an even greater energy source, such as that found in electrical storms (lightning), would demonstrate that electricity is quite capable of travelling quite considerable distances through air. There is not really a set of materials that are conductors and a set that are not, though some are much better than others. Metals will conduct electricity well, but again some will be better than others, especially over long distances.

An example of a non-metal conductor is graphite, a form of carbon. Its layered structure is such that the bonds between the layers are quite weak (the layers slide against each other making it a good lubricant) meaning that some of the electrons are quite loosely bonded. It is these electrons that allow the flow of electricity (and heat). Saline (salty water) is also a fair conductor of electricity. Common salt consists of the elements of chlorine and sodium, which is a metal. In the form of salt crystals, the bonding process prevents the flow of electrons, but when dissolved in water some of the sodium becomes free allowing the solution to conduct.

Magnetism

There are different forms of magnetism, only one of which, **ferromagnetism**, is useful in terms of testing and classifying the properties of materials in a primary school experiment. Magnets attract magnetic materials. These magnetic materials are either iron-based (an alloy containing iron) or are themselves magnets (magnets can be made from a non-metallic material called magnadur). It is therefore possible to sort metals by their attraction to a magnet. Ferromagnetism is the form of magnetism that allows a magnetic field (perhaps induced by an electrical current flowing through a coil) to be retained by a ferromagnetic material (such as iron, nickel, cobalt and their alloys).

'Static' charge, which can build up in non-metallic materials such as rubber and nylon, can also exert an attractive force. Party tricks use this phenomenon – 'sticking' balloons to walls, or using a nylon comb that has recently been used to comb hair, to 'bend' the flow of water from a tap. Although quite similar in effect, this is not ferromagnetism, it is a form of electricity resulting in the build-up of opposite charges. It should be noted that some types of stainless steel, due to the cooling process that they go through and the effect this has on the electron arrangements in the metal, are non-magnetic even though they are iron-based.

Absorbency

This property relates directly to the structure of the material and the 'gaps' that it contains between its fibres or granules (I hesitate to use the term 'particles' because these lumps are not really of that small, molecular scale). In much the same way that air can become 'trapped' by an insulating material, water can also permeate into the gaps in some circumstances. In some cases the material will expand as it absorbs more water whereas other, more rigid, materials will not. Powdered mashed potato will expand as it absorbs water while limestone will not.

The surface of an absorbent material tends to be dull and possibly rough, an indication that there are access points for water to get into the material. Absorbency is possible because the molecules of water are small enough to get between the particles in the structure of the solid material. It is, on a much smaller scale, similar to what happens when you mix a litre of marbles with a litre of dry, fine sand. When you pour the two into a larger container it will not reach the two-litre mark, as the sand will disperse itself between the marbles.

'Known' properties

There are occasions where a particular property can be noted but for which it is very difficult to objectively test. A good example of this is the distinction between manufactured and natural materials. The difficulty again comes from the object/material question.

Wood, for example, is a natural material, and when it is used in the production of manufactured objects – such as chairs – it remains a natural material. However, when wood, which has been turned into chips as part of the sawing process, is combined with glue and compressed into board to form chipboard, it becomes a manufactured material. All materials that have undergone a chemical change from their natural state are known as manufactured materials. These materials will include plastics, metals (that have been smelted from ore), ceramics (chemically changed clay) and wood-based products such as papers.

It is often difficult to identify and distinguish between natural and manufactured materials – frequently materials are manufactured to mimic the qualities of a natural material. Tests to determine the nature of materials are often quite involved, relying upon reactions with particular chemicals or the effects of exposure to heat or flame. Manufactured fabrics will often melt, for example, while their 'natural' counterparts will burn – but this rule varies far too much for it to become an objective test and, more importantly, it is not a very safe test. It eventually becomes a matter of 'knowing', and so depends on small, observable differences often based upon factors such as smell, texture or elasticity.

The ability to distinguish between materials on the basis of their physical characteristics is fundamental to the further study of materials science. In a broader sense it is also an essential element of being able to successfully navigate our way around in the modern world. The increasing everyday use of different materials encourages a greater knowledge of their characteristics, for example the use of different fabrics for clothing.

Why you need to know these facts

Vocabulary

Brittle – a material that breaks suddenly when a force is applied to it.
Elastic – a material that returns to its original shape following deformation.
Ferromagnetism – a form of magnetism that can lead to magnetism being retained to make a permanent magnet.
Hard – a material that is difficult to scratch or dent.
Opaque – blocks light.
Plastic – a material that does not return to its original shape following deformation.
Tough – a material that breaks slowly and in parts when a force is applied to it.
Translucent – allows light but not coherent images through.
Transparent – allows images through.

Properties of materials

- The most absorbent material is called 'H-span' which is capable of holding 1300 times its own mass in water – this is like a 2g paper kitchen towel being able to absorb 2.5 litres of water!
- The densest element commonly found on Earth is osmium – with a density of 22.8gcm^{-3}.
- The least dense solid is a silica aerogel (strands of silica and oxygen atoms) which can be manufactured with a density of approximately 0.005gcm^{-3}.
- The hardest known substance is carbon – but only when it has the crystalline structure of a diamond.
- 1 gram of gold can be stretched into a strand 2.4km long!

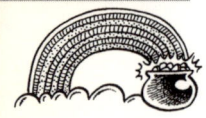

Metals are cold or if you leave them in the Sun they can feel very hot.

The temperature sensors in your skin perceive the temperature so well with metals because metals are an excellent conductor of heat. If the piece of metal is cold, heat will flow extremely well from your hand to the metal, giving you a very quick impression of 'coldness'. A different material, such as wood, can be just as cold as the metal, but because wood is such a poor conductor of heat it will be a few seconds before it actually feels cold – and by then your hand will have warmed that portion of the wood.

Wrapping frozen food in a jumper will make it warm up quicker.

Children don't always recognise that the insulation qualities of certain materials that are used to retain heat in one set of circumstances, can also be used to keep things cold in another. It is their ability to prevent the transfer of heat, to thermally insulate one area from another, which allows them to perform both tasks. Objects will revert to the ambient temperature of their environment if they are not insulated from it, so any material that is capable of thermally insulating an object from the surrounding environment should be just as good at keeping something hot as it is at keeping it cold. An ice lolly left in a warm room will melt and warm until it has reached room temperature – there will also be a marginal fall in the temperature of the room, as heat is transferred from the room to the lolly. On the other hand, wrapping a cold child in a thick woolly jumper will help them to warm up as they produce heat and the jumper helps retain it.

Why does paper (and fabric) get darker when wet?

Brighter colours reflect more and absorb less light than duller/darker ones. When paper or fabric gets wet, the water also absorbs some of the light falling upon it so there is less to reflect back to the viewer. Some materials, such as a stone, may become shiny when wet. This is due to the water forming a layer over the stone and the surface of the water reflecting light when it strikes it at an appropriate angle – that's why we get reflections off the surface of a pool.

Why does white paper (or fabric) become transparent when wet?

The first thing to say is that it doesn't become transparent in a similar way to clear glass, but images can be seen through it in a similar way to tracing paper. The white colour means that the material scatters all colours of light. When it gets wet, just as described above, more light is absorbed. Rather than turning black, the light that is absorbed goes through the material and is reflected back off what is underneath. If there is an object directly under the wet, white paper or fabric, an image of it will be seen just as with tracing paper. The thicker the fabric or paper is, the less of an image will be visible – so if you must have a white swimming cozzie, make sure that it's a nice thick one!

Observing materials (observing and describing)

Even restricting the children to purely visual and tactile observations, this form of activity can be performed at many different levels and organised in several different ways. The key focus is to build up a word bank of adjectives ('hard', 'shiny', 'translucent', 'elastic', 'fibrous', 'ductile') to define and describe different materials and refine observations at the same time. As a class or group teacher-led activity, the children will be offered several different examples of the same material. It is useful to begin by discussing the items to confirm that they are examples of the same material. The children then offer words to describe the material and discuss whether or not the term can apply to all of the examples (do they need to make sub-sets?). These words are then recorded. The same is done for other materials, each time going back to previous lists to assess similarities and differences. Children will frequently use their 'knowledge' about the materials, saying 'it's wood' – but what makes it wood? – what collection of physical characteristics defines it as wood? In this way the children can be encouraged to focus on the physical properties rather than their knowledge about the material.

Another way to approach this activity is for the children to work in pairs. One child describes the material that they are holding and the other has to pick that material out from a tray in front of them containing several different materials (so that describing the *object* won't help). The one with the tray must ask questions to try to narrow down the material that the other person is holding. It is interesting to observe how frequently the children will resort to their knowledge of the material rather than their observations – 'it's a plastic' or 'it's used for making scissors'! With older, more experienced children, the level of difficulty can be increased by having a collection of similar materials to work with – for example, only metals, or woods, or plastics. Clearly at least some preliminary work with the children will be required to ensure that at least they are able to identify (name) some of the materials being used.

The 'feely' box (observation, comparison)
Once visual observation has been removed from the 'armoury' it can make the task of identifying materials particularly challenging – but not impossible. 'Feely' boxes are used to identify objects by touch. To avoid focusing on the shape of the objects and promote concentration on the type of material, all of the examples offered in the bag should be of a similar size and shape. To make the task more achievable for the child, there should be two of each sample – one that might be placed in the feely box, and one that is put on the tray of 'possibles' with which the tester can compare. If the children have difficulties, hints can be given – the density of the material can be judged, and so can thermal conductivity, hardness and surface texture, by touch alone.

Shape changing (exploring, vocabulary recognition)
Using a lump of play dough, or similar modelling medium, encourage the children to carry out shape-changing actions. The teacher can offer a lead by giving the verb which the group of children then respond to by performing this on the play dough in front of them, or the words can be placed on cards. In this version a child may read the card, without showing the rest of the group, and perform the action on his or her play dough, leaving the group to guess the verb. Suggested verbs: twist, press, bend, scratch, dent, squash, stretch and so on.

Collections (observing, sorting)

Use a range of materials that may either be quite different or have significant similarities (for example, all metals). The children are asked to sort the materials into sets or an order based upon the properties of the materials. The classifications can either be pre-set (on cards which the teacher either matches to the capabilities of the children or which the children choose randomly) or defined by the children themselves. This can be performed as a relatively unsupervised activity with the children reporting back at the end. Alternatively, each week or for each group, the children may be asked to search and collect materials with a different specific property (for example, translucent) for a class display. Clearly, having a range of materials in the school in the first place as particularly good examples of particular properties is a very useful thing.

Testing electrical conductivity (observing, testing)

Children can individually or in small groups test different materials for electrical conductivity. By building a testing circuit (see Figure 3) children can complete the circuit using different materials and observe the outcome. For the sake of safety, children should not randomly test things around the classroom – obviously, it is important that they do not come into contact with mains electricity.

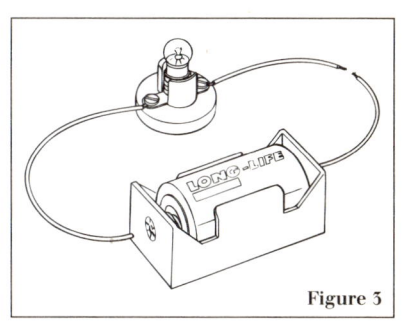

Figure 3

Magnetic attraction (observing, testing)

Children can individually or in small groups test different materials for their attraction to magnets. A permanent alnico magnet would be the most appropriate choice. Once the materials have been sorted into sets they might also be tested for their electrical conductivity – all materials attracted to magnets will also conduct electricity, but not vice versa. It is worth noting that the object chosen to represent a material must not have an outer coating of a different material – the paint on the outside of a steel tin will not prevent it from being attracted to the magnet but may significantly affect the electrical conductivity.

Thermal conductivity 1 (observing, testing, measuring)

Children can individually or in small groups test different materials for thermal properties. There are several different ways of doing this depending on the availability of resources. In the simplest format, a collection of spoons of equal size but made from different materials (steel, wood, plastic...) are placed in a cup of hot water. The spoon handles are regularly touched to gauge the extent to which the heat from water has been conducted – in this instance, thermometers would be very difficult to use accurately. A small knob of margarine or butter placed on the top of each spoon would also be a useful indicator – as the heat is conducted the fat will melt and slide down the spoon. If resources allow, identical strips of different materials can replace the spoons. An alternative approach would be to use cups made from different materials, smearing small knobs of margarine on the outside of the cups below the 'water lines'. Finding near identical cups, in terms of thickness and so on, may be very difficult. However, this is a particularly good way of finding out which type of vending machine hot beverage cup will cause you least pain when you grab hold of it!

Thermal conductivity 2 (observing, testing, measuring)

Whether you are attempting to get frozen foods home from the supermarket before they defrost, or fish and chips home before they cool down, the problem is the same. What do you wrap the items in to maintain their temperature? There are two ways for groups of children to approach this. Either they can use identical ice cubes and wrap them in different potential insulating materials (the same amount of material for each one to keep it fair) and compare remaining ice cubes after a short while. Or they can pour the same amount of hot tap water into identical fizzy drinks cans, each wrapped in a different insulating material. Use of these cans is recommended as they usually are manufactured from particularly conductive materials – and if they are knocked over, the small hole prevents too much from spilling out. Thermometers can be placed in the differently insulated cans and measurements taken at regular intervals. It is best to do this in a reasonably cold place to make the temperature difference between the water and the environment as great as possible. Even better, a temperature probe, connected to a remote sensing device on a computer, can be used to collect the data continuously and present the results graphically.

Density (observing, testing)

More than ever, it is important here that the children focus on the material, rather than on the shape in which it might be found. To test for density, relative to water, the materials need to be submerged in the water. If they rise to the surface then they are less dense, if they sink to the bottom then the material must be denser than water. As an extension for the more mathematically able, children can be asked to calculate the 'specific gravity' of materials that are denser than water. Use a spring balance to measure the weight of a piece of material, then repeat the weighing process with the piece of material submerged in water (see Figure 4). The weight in air is then divided by the weight in water to give the specific gravity of the material.

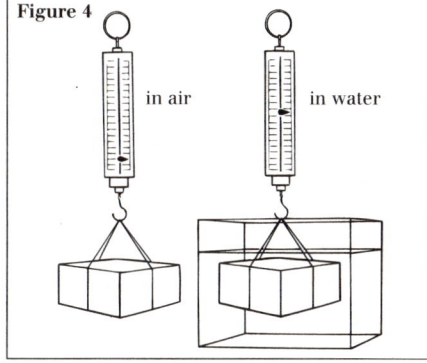

Figure 4   in air   in water

Hardness 1 (observing, testing)

Children may place a collection of different materials in order of hardness by assessing how easily they can be scratched. This is most easy to judge by attempting to scratch one material with another. The harder of the two materials will probably not be marked whilst the other will either be scratched or worn where the attempt was made to scratch the other material. By methodically working through the collection, the materials can be placed in order of softest to hardest. Orders confirmed by different children for the same materials can be compared, as can 'overlapping' collections of materials.

Hardness 2 (observing, testing)

To dent materials children must first start with an object hard enough to do the denting – a large steel ball bearing will probably do the trick. The ball bearing will be dropped from a height on to the material. To keep this process safe, the material should be placed on a cutting board on the floor (see Figure 5) and the ball bearing should be dropped down the centre of a card tube (the inner from a roll of carpet would be ideal) from a height of 1 to 1.5m. Carefully examine the surface of the material before the ball is dropped and then observe again afterwards. Not all of the materials will be marked, but those that are can be placed in order

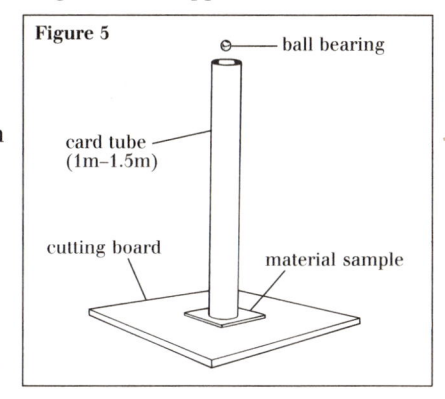

Figure 5   ball bearing

card tube (1m–1.5m)

cutting board   material sample

of deformation. It should be noted that only plastic materials will show lasting evidence of being dented – a piece of rubber will be dented but it will quickly revert to its original shape. Other materials may be so brittle that rather than denting (deforming), they crack (shatter). These materials, including glass and ceramic, are hard.

Deformation – stretching (observing, testing, measuring)

When asking children to stretch different materials by suspending different masses from them it is important to consider safety.

● Don't use large masses or pieces of material.

● Don't suspend the masses too far above the ground.

● Don't suggest materials that are going to snap and twang back in someone's face (such as steel wire or nylon fishing line).

● It's probably safest either to use goggles or to place a card tube around the material.

There are three key points to observe when performing such tests. First it is important to note whether the material stretches at all, then how much force is required to make it stretch and finally whether it returns to its original size once the force has been removed. Is it flexible? How flexible is it? Is it elastic or plastic? These three questions can be answered in one test – as long as the material sample is not tested to destruction! Using either of the set-ups suggested in Figure 6,

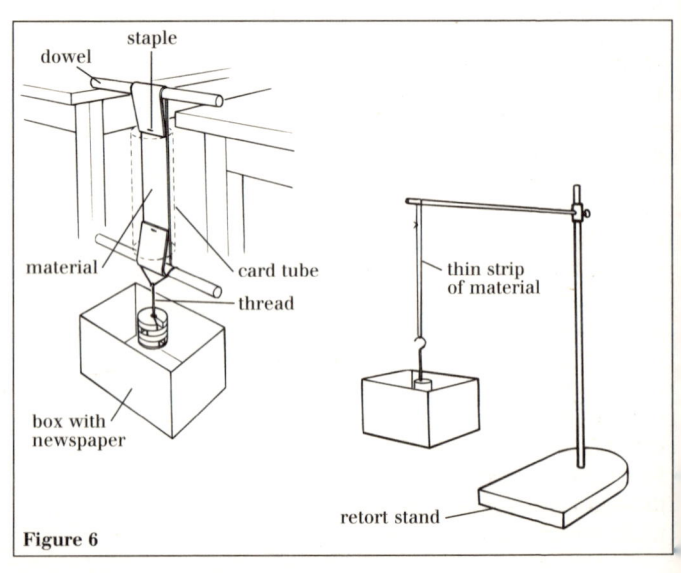

Figure 6

ensure that the material samples are small enough to be affected by the relatively small forces that the children will be able to safely apply. If the children are able to record the additional length to which the material has stretched for each additional mass then the tabulated results can be turned into a line graph. With certain materials, such as strips of plastic from supermarket shopping bags, it is important to cut strips perpendicular to each other and test them separately as they may stretch more in one direction than another.

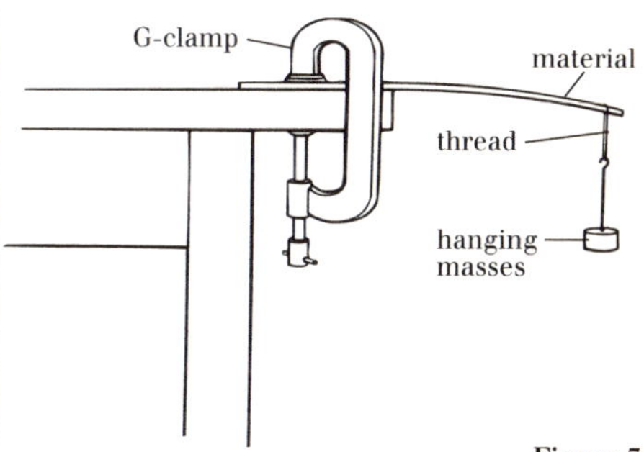

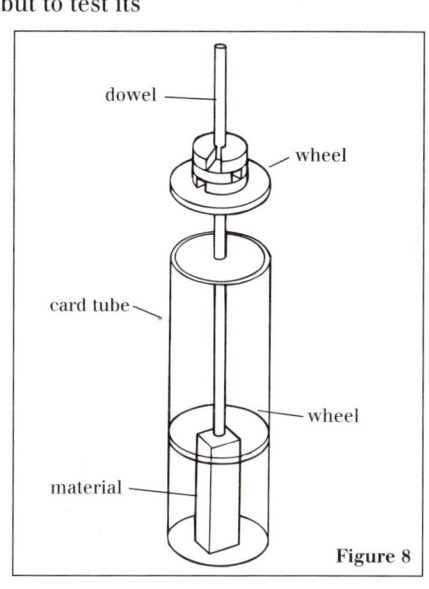

Figure 7

Deformation – bending (observing, testing, measuring)

Following the same safety guidelines as above, the children need to work in small groups to assess the flexibility of different 'stiff' materials (see Figure 7).

Again, efforts should be made to establish the degree of elasticity or plasticity of the materials. The same sized samples of materials should be used to allow for ease of comparison, and the samples themselves should be as thin as possible to allow the children to use relatively small masses to obtain their results. It is important that the children realise that the aim of the test is not to break the sample, but to test its flexibility.

Deformation – compression (observing, testing, measuring)

Once again, following the safety guidelines given above, the children can work in small groups to assess the affects of 'squashing' forces on different materials. It is quite difficult to actually test compression (see Figure 8) as small material samples are apt to crumple rather than be compressed. It would be sensible to choose only materials that will compress, and relatively small forces in the first place; samples of different types of foam or sponge or modelling media would be ideal.

Figure 8

Brittle or tough? (observation, inference)

Working with samples of broken pieces of material under supervision (the breaks can be very sharp) the children observe the fractures and use their knowledge to suggest whether the material is tough (splintered, jagged or rough break) or brittle (clean break).

Transparency/translucency/opaqueness (observation, testing)

When children test these qualities of a material they will have to work together in small groups and agree opinions. Which one can you see through best? Which one lets the least or the most light through? Transparent/translucent materials can be compared side by side in sunlight by using a lamp to see how much light they let through – or rather how dark a partial shadow they form. From this direct comparison, the materials can be placed in order of the one that lets the most light through to the one that is most opaque.

Absorbency (planning, observation, testing)

Groups of children design a 'fair test' in order to compare the absorbency of different, similar materials (different types of fabric or paper). They will need to consider how they will keep all of the samples the same (area or mass for example) and how they will compare (rank order, volume of water or change in mass ...) the outcomes.

Concept 2: The structure of materials

Subject facts

Using models

The particular nature of matter is clearly not a concept that is included in primary science, but so many of the explanations behind much of the work done at this stage with materials is based on this. These molecular models will be introduced early in Key Stage 3 so it is likely that some more able children would be ready for such ideas and any child working towards Level 6 would find them essential.

This section will take the opportunity to revisit the material properties addressed in the previous concept area and explain them in molecular terms.

Elasticity

Materials that are described as 'elastic' (they return to their original shapes) frequently have one of two types of structure. In the first type (see Figure 9), the materials are composed of long, chain-like molecules (**polymers**) which

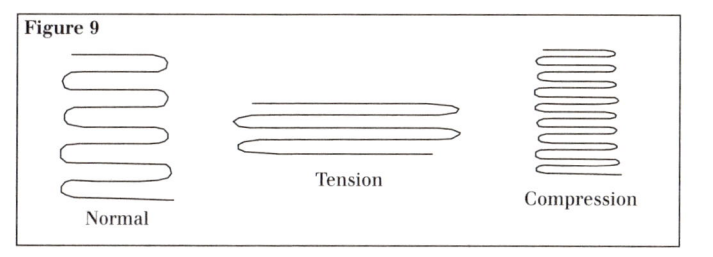

Figure 9

Normal

Tension

Compression

are normally quite 'scrunched-up'. When the material is placed under tension (stretched) the chain straightens out until it reaches its maximum extension. When the molecules in the material reach this point it is known as the 'elastic limit'. When the material is released, the molecules revert to their scrunched-up positions. If the material is stretched beyond this point, bonds between molecules will begin to be broken and the material will no longer be able to return to its original shape and size. In compression, the molecules are forced to scrunch up even more but will spring back to their original positions when released.

Other materials, often the more rigid ones, have a more regular molecular structure, with their atoms being held in quite uniform structures. The bonds between these atoms are strong and they attempt to retain their positions. In tension the bonds between the atoms will be stretched but only by relatively small amounts before the bonds break. In compression, the atoms will be forced closer but will immediately repel each other to regain their original distances – creating a 'bounce'. On rigid surfaces, steel ball bearings bounce particularly well.

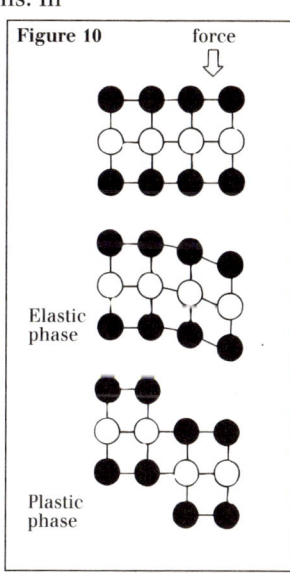

Figure 10

force

Elastic phase

Plastic phase

Plastic

The ability to reform in a different shape can be achieved in several ways. The two most common result from the malleability of certain metals and the mix of different materials in modelling media. The bonds within metals are interesting in many ways, not least because they are often initially elastic but, when forced to displace more, become plastic. When atoms are displaced (see Figure 10) they remain elastic to begin with – if they are released after a relatively small movement they will fall back into place. If they go beyond this point then the old bonds will break and new ones will form, fixing the material in its new position and shape. It will once again be in an elastic position and will bounce back to this new position if bent a small amount further. The elastic and plastic ranges vary considerably from metal to metal.

Most plastic modelling media are a mixture of solid particles and a lubricant. When clay is in its plastic form it consists of particles of clay held together and lubricated by water. Both plasticine and play dough are a mixture of particles (flour in the case of play dough) and oil (see Figure 11).

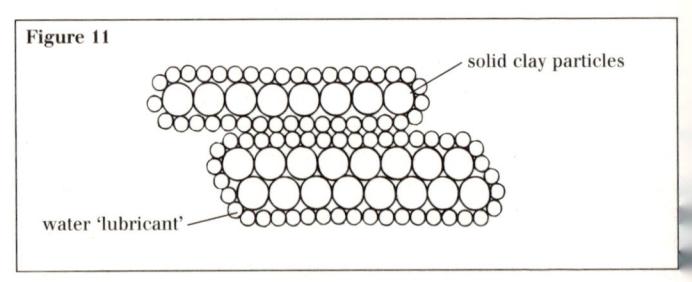

Figure 11

solid clay particles

water 'lubricant'

The solid particles are surrounded by a thin layer of liquid which allows the solid parts to be moved in relation to each other. Once the material has been reshaped, the new arrangement is held. In the case of play dough there is some 'springiness' within the material. This is mainly due to the nature of the flour particles which are made up of rather elastic, long-chain molecules. When the liquid is removed, for example when clay dries, the material becomes hard and breaks rather than bends. The way that these materials behave when they change is further explained in Chapter 5 'Chemical changes'.

Brittle

Almost all materials that are solid and brittle at room temperature have a similar structure based upon ionic bonding. This allows them to form giant structures – at least 'giant' in atomic terms! The actual ionic bonding process is explained on page 20. These structures have a crystalline uniformity to them, with bonds repeating themselves throughout the material. Some of the strongest materials that possess this giant structure are based upon covalent bonding rather than ionic. A good example of a covalent giant structure is a diamond (see Figure 12).

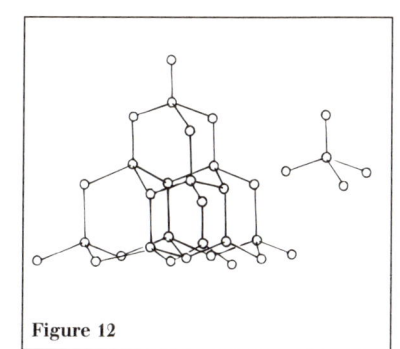

Figure 12

This is based upon a regular, three-dimensional bonding of carbon atoms. In a diamond, each carbon atom shares its electrons with four other carbon atoms, forming strong, attractive bonds with each. These bonds are very difficult to break, but when this does happen, usually along 'flaws' or planes of natural weakness, the diamond will be cleaved into different pieces. In most cases, though, covalent bonding only produces small molecules of only a few atoms bonded together.

The more easily shattered giant structures are based upon the weaker attractive forces of ionic bonding. These bonds (Figure 13) are based upon the attractive forces of opposite charges caused by an electron transferring from one atom to another. The atom that loses an electron will now have a positive charge and the one that gains will have a negative charge, which keeps the structure together, as long as the opposite charges are aligned. If the material is struck, or an external force is applied, the molecules may become displaced so that particles

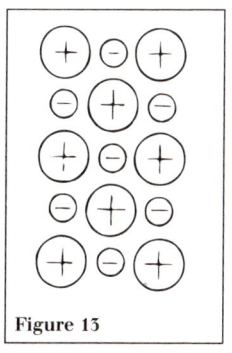

Figure 13

with the same charge now find themselves next to each other. The forces now between them are repulsive rather than attractive. The material will break apart along that plane.

In the case of a brittle material such as glass (based on ionic bonding – but a little more complicated than that!), it will be strong and rigid up to the point where molecules are displaced along a plane and the pane shatters. This is why it

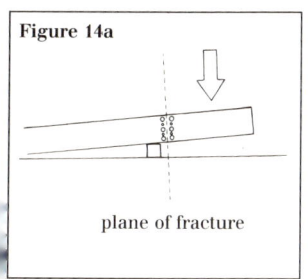

Figure 14a

plane of fracture

is possible to break glass (and glazed tiles) using relatively little force once a 'fault plane' has been established. By scoring the surface of the brittle material with a hard, sharp implement, to cause a scratch (Figure 14a), a relatively small force to 'bend' the material at that point will cause it to fracture and the weakness is transmitted through the material (see Figure 14b).

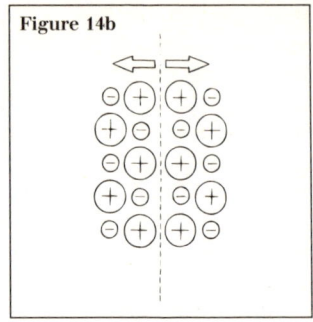

Figure 14b

Composite materials, such as concrete, bricks and compacted earth, are particularly brittle, especially under tension because of the weakness of the bonding agents between the particles. As long as they are kept in place, and under compression, they are fine, otherwise they are subject to sudden breaks. To avoid this problem of brittleness, particularly in concrete, the material can be strengthened by the addition of a material that is strong in tension – steel in reinforced or 'pre-stressed' concrete.

Some plastics, such as polystyrene (the clear variety used for making rulers, not the expanded polystyrene used for packing), is made up of molecule chains based upon atoms of carbon and hydrogen. These tend to line up so that, although the material is fairly flexible, when it is pushed beyond a particular point, it will shatter along one of these planes where the ends of molecule chains are most dense. It is not brittle because of the bonds within the molecule but brittle because of the bonds *between* the molecules.

Tough

Materials that are tough have a degree of flexibility, even if it is only while they are in the process of breaking. Unlike the brittle materials above, they do not exhibit such a regular pattern in their structural bonding. This greater degree of 'randomness' prevents them from catastrophically failing along a particular line. There are two main ways that 'toughness' is exhibited within molecular structure. The first is when the material consists of a 'fibrous' arrangement of interconnected long-chain molecules; the second is when the material contains a molecular structure that is able to break and reform in a different arrangement a number of times before breaking.

Most plastics are tough materials, relying on the strength within their molecular structure to prevent them from easily breaking – polythene, for example, is based upon a chain of over 200 000 carbon atoms in each molecule. The toughness of these types of materials comes from the need to break each individual molecule apart from the ones next to it to separate one piece of the material from another. That is why when you rip a polythene bag it will stretch and thin considerably before it finally comes apart. Even when you start a break by cutting into the material with a sharp implement, the break will not be continued. An organic material such as wood provides a fine example of toughness on a much larger scale. The fibres are large enough to be seen. The breaking of these fibres, prior to the piece of wood breaking into two, is audible and can actually be 'felt' as the piece of wood begins to 'give' and weaken. This can be used as a model of what happens at a molecular level in tough, non-metallic materials.

Metals can also be described as 'tough' but they cannot be described as having a 'fibrous structure'. In fact, metals have a crystalline structure, which would suggest, given the previous section, that metals should be brittle. Well, some are – such as cast iron – but the key element is that they do not break upon a clean plane like glass and ceramic. If you were to see the surface of a piece of metal along where it had broken it would be very rough – but it would give a very strong impression that it had a crystal-like structure. When a piece of metal breaks through fatigue (usually caused by a constant vibration which causes a crack to develop and spread through the material) the exposed surface will show where the weak links were in the atomic structure of the material. Just bending a metal, unless it has a particularly coarse crystalline structure (as in the case with cast iron) will cause the bonds to break and reform – moving through the elastic and plastic phases described above. If this bending takes place while the metal is hot, a strong crystalline structure will reform and the strength of the metal will be the same. If the bending takes place when it is cold, it will become much more brittle about that area and will eventually break if it is re-bent further there. See for yourself by repeatedly bending a steel paper clip.

Conductivity

The generally perceived (well, at least among scientists) view of the structure of a conductor, such as a metal, is that it is a fairly regular (giant or crystalline) structure made up of ions (the positively charged nuclei of the atoms) in a 'sea' of electrons. As described earlier, the special thing (well, *one* of the special things) about metals is that the outer electron shell is nearly empty, so that the electrons are not particularly strongly attached to 'their' atom. The electrons from the outer shells of these atoms are therefore visualised as randomly wandering from the influence of one atom to the influence of another, within the piece of metallic material. Aluminium, for example, has 13 electrons. These are arranged in three shells: two in the first, eight in the second – making each of them 'complete' – and the remaining three in the third shell. As this outer shell is five electrons short of being complete, these three electrons will wander from atom to atom. Conductivity is all about the transfer of energy from one place to another and within a material – these wandering electrons make an excellent transport system.

In the case of heat, there is a transfer of energy at the surface of the material. Consider the situation where a piece of metal has been left in the sunshine. The light from the Sun strikes the surface of the metal – or more accurately **photons** (particles of light energy) strike the metal. When this happens, the energy in the photons is transferred to the electrons in the metal. The electron will either re-emit a photon (of a different energy level) allowing you to see the piece of metal or absorb the energy, causing it to become 'excited'. Basically, when the electron gets excited we perceive it as 'getting warmer'. Because these electrons are able to wander between atoms in the metal, these excited electrons soon become dispersed, warming the metal as a whole (see Figure 15). The more photons that strike the metal, the more electrons there will be in this excited state and the warmer the metal will feel. Essentially the freely moving electrons allow the heat to be spread throughout the material relatively quickly. If you touch the now-warmed piece of metal, the heat will rapidly pass into you as these electrons lose their energy to your hand. As the electrons are still flowing, they will come into contact with your hand, give up their energy and move off to be replaced by another electron ready to give up its energy.

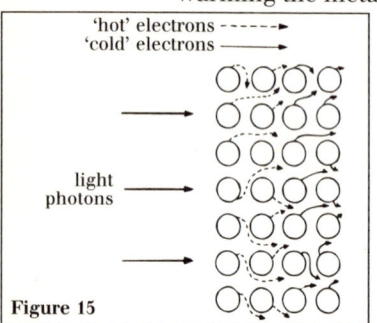

'hot' electrons ------►
'cold' electrons ——►

light photons

Figure 15

An insulator, on the other hand, without these freely moving electrons, will not be able to spread the energy throughout the material as quickly, so the warmth will build up only slowly as one atom slowly transfers energy to the next. Once the energy level (warmth) of this material has built up, it will be equally reluctant to cool down. When you touch an equally warm material that is an insulator, it will be the same temperature but it won't feel as hot (at least not immediately) because the energy transfer from the material to your hand will not be as fast.

The transmission of electricity within a conducting material is also due to these 'free electrons', but rather than just wandering randomly they are being encouraged to move in a particular direction. All electrical flow of this nature must be as part of a closed circuit (see Figure 16). When an electrical cell, a device that employs a chemical reaction to convert chemical energy into a flow of electrons, is connected in a circuit with a conductor, electrons are encouraged to flow in a particular direction due to the transfer of electrons in the chemical reaction. In the case of direct current, as supplied by a battery, the flow is always in one direction. With alternating current, the electrons first flow in one direction, then back the way that they came – in the case of mains electricity, this reversal happens 50 times per second.

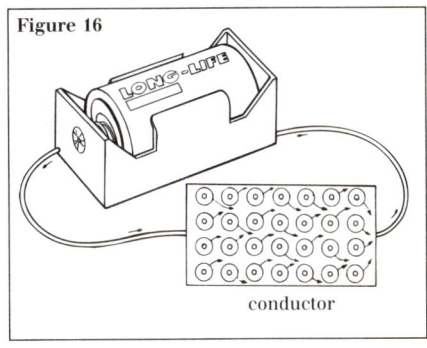

Figure 16

conductor

In non-conducting materials (almost all non-metals) the attachment of electrons to their atoms prevents the *easy* flow of electricity but cannot prevent it entirely. If the electrons are flowing into the material with sufficiently high energy levels they can force their way through. A small 1.5V battery contains relatively small amounts of stored energy so that if you touch both terminals at the same time, the electrons will not be able to flow. A battery that you might find in a car contains considerably more energy and will be able to force electrons to flow through your body – playing havoc with the small electrical flows in your body that control and operate muscles. There is sufficient energy in the flow of mains electricity to cause considerable damage as the electrons flow through your body disrupting the atoms in your body. In the case of lightning, so much energy is involved that the air is ionised – an electron is ejected from atoms of gases within the air giving them an overall positive charge which will allow electricity (electrons) to flow through them. The electrons can then flow along these pathways of ionised air. The amount of energy involved in lighting is so great that as the electrons flow through the ionised gases they literally blow the gas molecules apart.

Transparency

The differences between transparent, translucent and opaque materials explained in terms of their atomic structures are very complicated. To explain these properties in these terms means that we have to go beyond the simple (!) 'scattering' model described on pages 29–30. At an atomic level, light does not exist in the same way that we perceive it – it has to be treated as a form of energy particle.

The first key point that you need to accept is the relationship between photons (the little packets of light energy, remember) and electrons. As mentioned above in the conductivity section (page 50), when photons strike the surface of a piece of material they normally interact with the electrons in the atoms of that material, moving the electrons to a higher energy level. Electrons, it has been found, can only exist at particular energy levels, and these levels are equivalent to the different 'shells' at which electrons can be found around the nucleus of the atom. In most circumstances when a photon strikes an electron it will give the electron sufficient energy to 'jump' to the next energy level (shell) – in effect this is the act of absorption (warming the material up). At the same time as the electron moves up an energy level it will also emit a photon of a particular energy level or colour as we would perceive it. The more energy the original photon transferred to the electron in the first place, the more blue or violet the colour of light finally emitted will be. The less energy originally transferred the redder the light will be (see Figure 17).

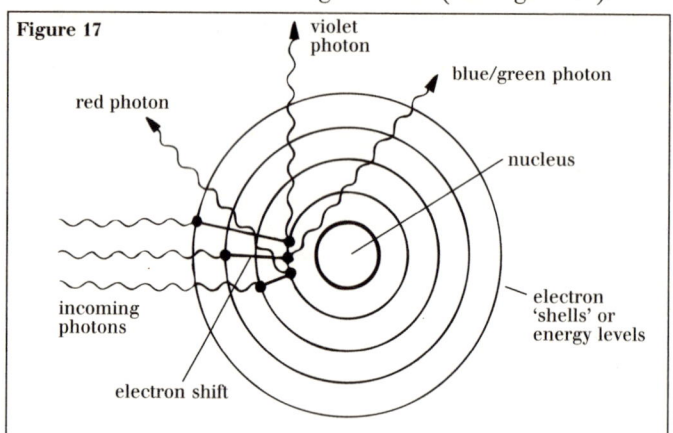

Figure 17

violet photon

blue/green photon

red photon

nucleus

incoming photons

electron 'shells' or energy levels

electron shift

On a sub-atomic level this explains how we see objects made from opaque materials, not how some materials are transparent or translucent. The key thing to appreciate here is that the electrons in a transparent material do not interact with the photons striking them. This, on the face of it, can be a very difficult concept to grasp. It is saying that a particle of light does not interact with a lump of matter – quite dense matter (relatively speaking) in the case of glass, say. The question that the model must address is why light can traverse a lump of material like glass, but fails to do the same through expanded polystyrene, which clearly has a lot less 'stuff' in it. All matter mainly consists of space between the bits so there shouldn't be a problem about sneaking a small particle like a photon through – but we still come up with the problem of why some materials and not others. What do all of these transparent materials have in common?

The key element that they have in common is the arrangement of their electrons. In transparent materials the electrons are in shells (that is, at energy levels) that do not readily accept energy from photons. There is some transfer of energy, mainly at surface impurities or flaws in the material, so not all of the light entering the material goes through. The key is that the photons striking the material do not find any electrons with which they can interact and to which they can give

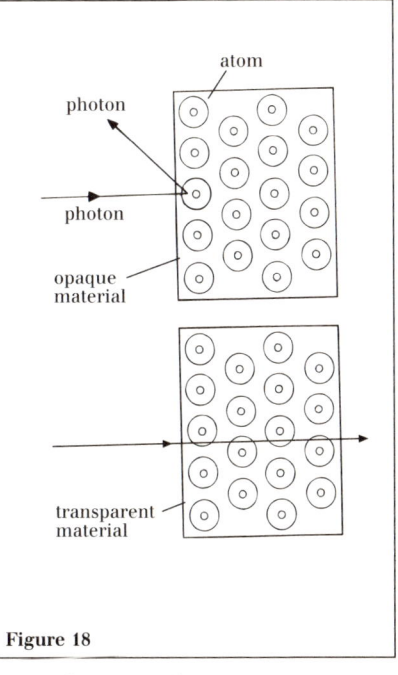

Figure 18

up their energy, so they simply continue on their way (see Figure 18). There is some slowing down of the photons as they enter denser transparent materials, so the angle at which they enter or leave is important because it will alter (refract) the direction of the light. In translucent materials some of the photons will interact with the electrons but many will not. Those that do not interact, at least to the extent that their energy is transferred to the electrons, will be transmitted through the material. Because of the structure of the material they will not travel straight through, as they would in a transparent material, but are scattered so that no clear image is visible on the other side.

Carbon – a special case

The carbon atom is remarkably versatile: it can be used in many different ways and can be found as the basis of many different materials. On its own, it can be commonly found in two different forms: graphite and diamond (okay, perhaps not *that* common!). Diamond, as shown previously in Figure 12, is a giant crystalline structure of carbon atoms, where every atom of carbon is bonded to four others in an immensely strong structure. Although graphite is a very different material, it is made from exactly the same atoms but arranged in a different way. In this material the carbon

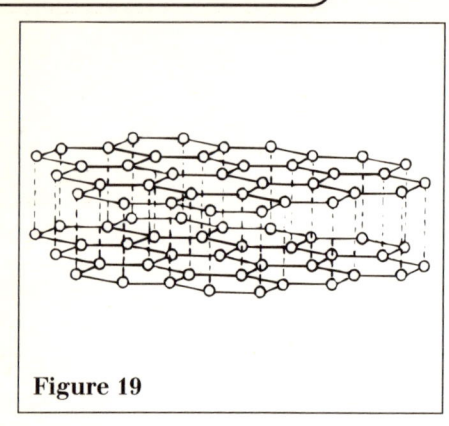

Figure 19

atoms are arranged in layers, with only weak bonds between them (see Figure 19).

In this arrangement, each carbon atom is bonded to three others in the same layer, and weakly to an atom in either the layer above or below. These weak bonds mean that in the outer shell of each of the carbon atoms there is an electron that is not firmly bonded. This allows the electron to 'wander' when it is given a push in the right direction, so graphite will conduct electricity (rather a rarity for a non-metal!) but will not conduct heat very well. As the layers are only loosely bonded they are capable of sliding in respect to each other – this makes graphite an excellent lubricant. Carbon can also exist in 'amorphous lumps' as it is able to double bond to other carbon atoms – that is, share two electrons with another carbon atom; each atom only needs to be in contact with two others for all shells to be completed through covalent bonding. These lumps are pretty irregular and of no great technological value.

A quite recently manufactured new form of carbon using atoms arranged in hexagons and pentagons, rather like a football, is buckminster fullerine (a carbon sphere). Although there aren't a great number of uses for it at the moment, it can be made into long thin tubes, which could either act as containers for other atoms, or as conductors in microscopic computer technology. The most useful purpose to which this basic form of carbon has been put is that it can be made into a helical shape – the basis of DNA (or life as we know it – we are carbon-based life forms after all!).

Why you need to know these facts

Quite often children will ask those 'why' questions that you will only be able to answer in the most general terms – not because you don't know or are not sure, but because the next level of understanding requires such a big jump. At these points it is important that you have a clear idea of what those next steps are so that you can lay realistic foundations for them. If you have a sound understanding of the models explaining the structures of materials in particular circumstances, there is a good chance that you can avoid instilling misconceptions leading to misunderstanding later in the children's educational careers.

Photon – a particle of light.
Polymer – a long molecule that is constructed of a 'chain' of atoms.

● The hardest known material, diamond, is also one of the most transparent.

Less dense materials have more air in them.
On a sub-atomic particle scale, the less dense the material the less matter (electrons, protons and neutrons) it contains, but this doesn't mean that there are gaps between the particles filled with air. At this level the particles in air are big! The space between the particles are filled with, well, space – the sort of space you get between solar systems, in other words, nothingness! There are materials, of course, that do contain air, such as sponge cake and expanded polystyrene, but these materials are mixtures with air, not uniform materials in their own right.

Concept 3: Selecting materials by their properties

Important properties

Are you sitting comfortably? Good – what is it that you are actually sitting on? What materials have been used to make this seating **artefact**? Why have they been chosen? Which others could have been used? Why weren't they in this case?

These questions give you a flavour of the importance of approaching materials from this perspective – materials are chosen for their uses.

Materials scientists or technologists test all materials in order to identify and quantify their physical properties. My DIY book tells me the comparative properties of different types of softwood, for example. From the table I can compare the relative merits of Scots pine, Baltic redwood, Douglas fir and western red cedar in terms of density,

compressive and tensile strength (with and against the grain), flammability, dimensional change with increasing moisture content, and their modulus of elasticity. Admittedly, I've had this book for over 20 years and I've never once wanted to know, in that detail, the relative characteristics of these woods – I tend to place myself in the 'best guess' school of DIY. People who do not subscribe to this school of thought (just about everybody who has to design and make something on a commercial basis presumably) tend to use such tables to ensure the most cost-effective use of materials to meet particular requirements. It is important to know, for example, if you intend to use stone slabs in a wet environment, such as a garden path, that while Portland stone (so my book tells me) absorbs 6–11% water, granite will only absorb 0.1– 0.5%. Why is this important to the would-be slab layer? If water gets in and then freezes, as it is apt to do in a garden, it will seriously damage the face of the stone, making it dangerous to walk on. Once the water freezes, it expands and forces the stone apart.

With regard to your seating artefact, or 'chair' for short, not only do we need to consider the aesthetics and **ergonomics** (and cost!), we also need to consider the relative merits of the materials used in the design. If we take a set of shelves, for example, there are several comparable materials from which they can successfully be manufactured. Indeed, from where I am seated at the moment I can see bookcases constructed from plastic covered **chipboard**, painted MDF (medium density fibreboard), pine, beech and mild steel sheet. Clearly all of these materials are capable of meeting the demands of use in the construction of shelving, so other factors (those mentioned above) come into play.

An approach that is often used to narrow down a wide range of materials to a more manageable number is to rank the desired properties. When beginning the process of choosing a material to fulfil a particular purpose it is helpful to identify all of the necessary properties required. Some will be more important or necessary than others so, to make the task of deciding easier, they can be ranked into three categories: essential, desirable and useful. For a material to pass through the first stage of the decision-making process it will need to exhibit all of the essential properties and the remaining materials can then be further narrowed down by reference to the secondary characteristics. To be effective, the criteria have to be very carefully chosen and applied.

Children will more often get to know materials by the objects that have been made out of them. They will quickly connect the properties required of the object with the properties that are possible from different materials. By making the process very practical, children will backtrack from the object to the properties exhibited by the materials that potentially might be used to construct the object. Children will begin to identify alternative materials which would satisfy the same needs, and thus begin to place the materials in a hierarchy of preference according to their secondary (economic, technological and availability) characteristics.

Why you need to know these facts

Artefact – a manufactured product.
Chipboard – a wood-based product manufactured by compressing wood chips and glue to make solid sheets.
Ergonomics – the study of humans and their interaction with their surroundings, in particular tools and furniture (how else could chairs be made so comfy?!).

Vocabulary

Glass is used in windows because it does not scratch very easily.
No – glass is used in windows because it is transparent! This is meant to cover a whole host of points, but is based around the observation that children will often miss the obvious reason for choosing a particular material. Aluminium is chosen for fizzy drinks cans primarily because it is impermeable, not because it is not attracted to magnets! Children need to focus on the essential properties before the desirable (or even irrelevant but interesting ones).

Common misconceptions

Why are ships and cars made out of metal?
Most ships used to be built out of wood, but wood only comes in relatively small pieces and has to be frequently treated to prevent it decaying. A key benefit of metal is that it can be joined together and sealed to prevent water getting in – sealing the joints between pieces of wood is much more difficult. Plastics, particularly fibreglass, have been used to make small boats for quite some time. As new types of plastic are developed, they will be used for more and more purposes – some ships and car parts that used to be made of metal (hulls and body panels) are now more often made of plastic, and this trend is likely to continue.

Questions

What are synthetic fabrics made from?

From nylon to Lycra, most synthetic fibres are made in chemical processes based upon oil, the same as all other plastics. All petroleum-based plastics are constructed of long chain molecules of mainly carbon and hydrogen. To make the fibres, the plastic is drawn out into long strands. They tend to be harder wearing and more elastic than most natural fibres.

Teaching ideas

Object properties (recording, sorting)

Take an object, such as a table or winter coat, and ask the class or group to brainstorm all of the properties that the object requires (for example, table: rigid, strong, hard). Then try to list all of the materials that exhibit those properties (either all or some). Discuss the relative merits of making the object out of those materials.

Material properties (identifying, recording)

Write the name of a material in the centre of a piece of paper. Around it list all of the properties that the material has. Around that, list some of the objects that are made from that material. Draw lines to link the most essential properties of that material to each object.

Properties (listing, recording)

Pick a property (such as absorbency, transparency, hardness) and have the children either individually or in groups list the materials that exhibit this property. List some objects that require this property and relate these to the materials.

Links (comparing)

Produce 10 to 20 cards each with the name of a different material written on it. The game is played in a small group. One card is placed face up on the table and the rest face down in a pile. The first player takes the top card off the pile and tries to think of a property that it shares with the card on the table. If a 'link' can be made it is placed on top. The next player then does the same until the pile is exhausted. If a link cannot be made, the player must keep the card. At the end of the game the player with the least cards 'wins'.

Guess what? (comparing, identifying)

Played along similar lines to 'Guess Who?'. Using two identical sets of the cards used for the 'links' game, a pair of children test their knowledge of material properties. One child chooses a material and the other has to guess which one it is by asking closed questions: 'is it hard?', 'is it opaque?'. Their own set of cards can be used to help them to narrow down the possibilities.

Resources

Material samples:
- ready broken pieces of, for example, wood, polythene, clay
- transparent, transluscent and opaque materials
- various fabric off-cuts and pieces of paper

Standard materials sets (identical blocks of different materials)

Sets of similar types of materials to test – for example paper, fabric, metals, woods, plastics, threads

Various elastic materials – such as rubber bands

Play dough and other modelling materials

Magnets

Bulb, battery and bulb holder (conductivity testing)

Fizzy drinks cans, thermometers (or remote data capture equipment)

Masses (for various 'strength' tests)

Websites
http://www.geocities.com/CapeCanaveral/Lab/5875/
This is the site for: Paul's Chemistry Lab: Chemistry Links for the Grade School Through Graduate School Student

Reference
Pocket Guides: Physical Processes by Neil Burton (Scholastic)

Chapter 3
CHANGING STATE

Key concepts

The observable process of the same substance changing from **solid** to **liquid** to **gas** as it is heated is exemplified by water. Unfortunately water is the only common chemical that does this at 'normal' temperatures. Helping children to distinguish between substances that will change their state on heating and cooling, and those that will not, will be an important distinction to make. The key ideas to be developed here are that:

1. There are different states of matter, namely solid, liquid and gas.
2. The changing state can be described in terms of the way atoms move in relation to each other.

Changing state concept chain

See 'The nature of "stuff" concept chain' on page 12 for general comments.

KS1
- Materials can be categorised as solid, liquid or gas.
- Water changes from solid to liquid to gas as it is heated.

KS2
- The three states of matter can be defined in terms of their ease of flow and maintenance of shape and volume.

● Not all materials are able to progress through all three states (for example, carbon dioxide sublimates from solid to gas).

● Water is one of the few substances that can exist in all three states at temperatures achievable in the classroom.

KS3

● Molecular models can be used to describe and explain the structural changes in substances changing from one state to another.

● Liquids and gases are collectively known as 'fluids'.

Concept 1: Solids, liquids and gases

Subject facts

Most children will have little difficulty in assigning the materials that they commonly have experience of to one of these three categories: solid, liquid and gas. Defining these categories in simple terms helps to lay firm foundations for future developments.

A material is said to be solid if it retains its shape, independently of anything around it. Although plastic and elastic materials can have their shapes changed they do have a definite shape – either the one to which they have been moulded or the one to which they return. Consequently, a solid material has nothing to do with how hard or rigid that it is, but everything to do with its retained shape. These factors can be explained in terms of the molecular structure of the material (see pages 44–8 and 'Changing states' below).

Liquids have a much more relaxed attitude to shape: they will happily accept the shape of the container into which they have been placed, or spread out across a level surface until they form a thin layer. Liquids can be poured, but different liquids flow at different rates – it is easier to spill milk than treacle. The resistance to flow of a liquid is known as its **viscosity** – the more viscous, the slower the rate of flow.

Gases are probably the hardest to define because, although we are surrounded by air, there are few safe, commonly available gases that can be seen as examples. Gases and liquids have the combined name of 'fluids' as they share many properties concerning flow. While a liquid will gather together in the bottom of a container, a gas will spread and thin out to fill a container (assuming that the container has a lid on). Also, a gas can be compressed to fill a smaller sized container, but a liquid, while it can be placed under pressure, is much more difficult to be made to take up a smaller volume. You can check this out for yourself by using a syringe or a balloon (see Figure 1).

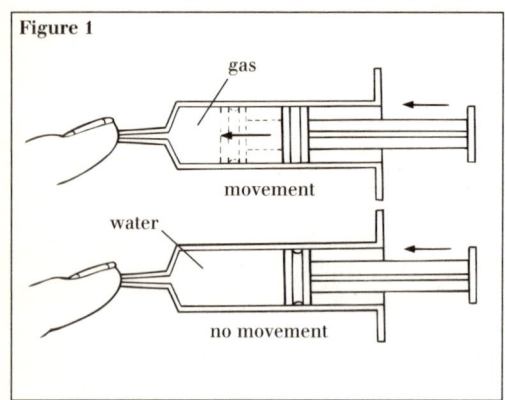

Figure 1

gas

movement

water

no movement

Compare water- and air-filled syringes (or balloons) for compressibility.

In the same way that small particles of a solid in water, such as table salt or flour, do not make the solid a liquid, small particles of a solid or liquid floating around in air do not make them a gas. Smoke (see 'Suspensions' on page 89) is made up of small particles suspended in the air. Visible water particles suspended in the air go by the names 'cloud', 'fog' or 'mist' – there is also a gaseous version of water in the air – vapour – but it is invisible (at least until it condenses on a cold surface).

Atomic structure

Solids, as described in Chapter 2 'Properties of materials', have a regular and relatively fixed particular arrangement – relatively, because most can be rearranged in one way or another by bending or otherwise reshaping. Plastic materials like putty, Plasticine and play dough can be reshaped, but once you have stopped fiddling with them and put them down, the particles in the material once more rigidly hold their positions. Elastic materials do resume their positions, but once they have done this they remain still. In terms of structure, at the atomic level, it is useful to

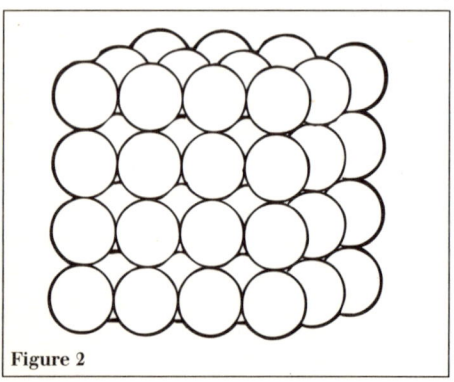

Figure 2

visualise solids as uniform and fixed arrangements of particles (see Figure 2). In different materials the arrangements (and types of atoms) will vary, but how they vary is not especially important here. Just imagine them as being pretty well fixed in place. Okay, I know I've already said that in metals electrons randomly wander from one atom to another, but in the states of matter we are considering the atoms themselves are fixed, not the sub-atomic particles.

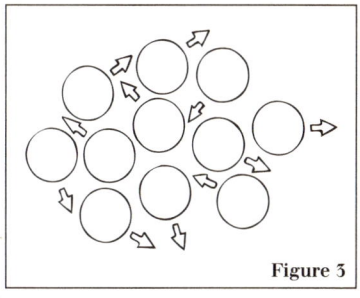

Figure 3

The molecules, uniform arrangements of atoms, that make up a liquid are not fixed in place relative to other molecules. They are able to move freely around – though their rate of movement does depend upon the viscosity of the liquid, that is, how easily the molecules slide past one another. In this case, the model to visualise (see Figure 3) is one where the molecules are still quite closely packed but able to move at random, relative to each other.

The movement of the molecules of a gas is much greater than the movements in a liquid. The gas particles tend to be further apart than a liquid (see Figure 4), which allows a gas to be compressed – halve the volume in which a given amount of gas is contained and the pressure that the gas exerts on the container will be doubled (this is known as 'Boyle's Law', after Robert Boyle's discovery in 1661).

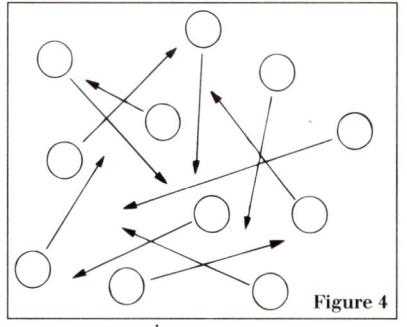

Figure 4

The differences between the three states can be explained in terms of the molecular movement. In Figures 2 to 4, the main differences are in the rates of movement relative to each other (okay, the length of the arrows representing movement!). This kinetic (movement energy) model of the states of matter is one that is explored in greater depth later as we examine the changes from one state to another.

Viscosity

This is the resistance to the flow of a liquid. Some liquids – clear honey is a good example – seem to move in slow motion. You have to wait for ages for it to fall from your spoon on to your piece of toast. Why?

In the act of pouring, a liquid will flow due to gravitational attraction. As you begin to pour, a layer of molecules at the top begins to flow in a particular direction and some of those molecules flow into the layer below and cause them to move. In a low-viscosity liquid, the layer below will readily accept this urge to flow, causing a cascade of the liquid. In a high-viscosity liquid, there is a great deal of interaction between the molecules that are moving and the ones that are stationary. The moving ones flow into the stationary ones and are slowed down, and the slow moving ones mingle with the flowing ones and slow them down, making the average speed of the liquid particularly sluggish. And the last drop of honey is still dripping from the spoon!

Sometimes warming the liquid will reduce the viscosity and make it easier to pour – golden syrup is a good example of this. You may have noticed how cooking oil will tend to form a quite thick pool in the centre of a frying pan when you first pour it in cold. As it heats up it will then spread out to form a much thinner layer as its viscosity reduces.

Why you need to know these facts

Children are aware of these terms but not necessarily in their true scientific form. An understanding of these states and how they are defined is an important step towards understanding the nature of matter and how it operates on a molecular level.

Vocabulary

Gas – a material that can spread out to fill an enclosed container.
Liquid – a material that adopts the shape of the bottom of a container.
Solid – a material that retains its shape.
Viscosity – the resistance to the flow of a liquid.

Amazing facts

● Hydrogen is the least dense gas – water is 10 000 times more dense than hydrogen gas at sea level atmospheric pressures.
● Radon, at sea level, is the densest simple gas – it is still only 1/100th the density of water (so there is the same difference between hydrogen and radon as radon and water)
● The viscosity of boiling water is about 30% of what it is at 20°C – that way you get a much better 'flow' around your potatoes so that they cook more evenly.

Common misconceptions

Gases smell.
Well, I have to agree that some do – and some smell better than others! But if you are always surrounded by something (air springs to mind) then your senses will become deadened to the smell and you will tend not to notice it after a while. Let's face it, if there was suddenly an absence of air around you, your first response would hardly be 'mmm, that smells different'.

All solids are regular shapes.
You can safely blame mathematicians for this misunderstanding. There are regular solids and there is the collection of properties which are known as 'solid'. Children just need to get to understand the different contexts in which we use the term and remember which definition they are using on this occasion.

Solids are hard.
We English-speakers have caused a problem for ourselves by giving the same word several very similar (but, importantly, not quite the same) meanings. The language can happily handle 'as solid as rock' but it will metaphorically raise an eyebrow at 'as solid as polystyrene'. I'm even apt to use the phrase 'that's more solid now' – usually after repairing something I'd made previously to a somewhat lower quality threshold – that refers to the strength and rigidity of an object. In the context of material classification, solids are solids – they retain their shapes, unless reshaped by an external force.

Questions

Is sand a liquid?
It may seem like a strange question but sand certainly flows like one, and it will take up the shape of a container. There are two significant differences though: if poured on to a surface it will form a mound and the particles are too large – they are broken bits of solid rather than small, molecular structures (see 'Changing states' below). Though each grain of sand is a solid, when dry, sand can flow like a fluid.

Are all liquids just different types of water?
Given the commonly found liquids around the home, particularly in the kitchen, this may very well be the experience of children. Milk, juice, cordial and fizzy drinks are all mainly water. Others, such as cleaning fluids and disinfectants are solutions (see Chapter 4 'Mixing and separating'). There are some key liquids that are chemically different from water, including fuels (petrol, diesel), lubricants (oil), fats (corn and olive oil) and a metal (mercury). None of these contain water – that is, molecules of H_2O.

Changing state

Solid, liquid or gas (observing, sorting, classifying)

Ask the children either individually, in groups or as a class to make a list of solids, liquids and gases that they know. Throw in some examples of your own (such as sand, salt, baby powder, fog, smoke) to test their understanding. Discuss their ideas.

Gases (research, recording)

Individually or in groups, children identify a gas (oxygen, methane, carbon dioxide ...) and use science CD-ROMs (for example, Dorling Kindersley's *Science Encyclopedia*) or the Internet to find out more about that gas. Present this information to the rest of the class.

Concept 2: Changing states

Subject facts

The state of matter and energy levels

Almost all pure or simple materials (such as water or steel), but not complex chemical mixtures like chocolate or wood, can be found in one of three states of solid, liquid or gas, depending upon their energy levels – basically, how hot they are. The reason that not all materials go through these reversible phases (both wood and chocolate burn at particular temperatures, for example) is that at certain temperatures the chemical mixtures of these substances react to form new materials (see Chapter 5 'Chemical changes'). For most of these pure or simple-structure materials, the majority of the time temperature is a good indicator of their energy levels. There are points where this is not the case – at **boiling** and **freezing** points – where a liquid changes into either a gas or a solid. At these points the energy change will cause a change in the state of the structure of the material rather than a change in temperature.

If water is heated, the temperature will continue to rise until it reaches 100°C, at which point the water will start to change into its gaseous form, steam. Adding extra energy in the form of heat at this stage will not increase the temperature, but will turn more of the liquid into **vapour**. Only when all, or at least most, of the water has turned to steam will the temperature begin to rise once more. The same discontinuity in the temperature rise will occur when heat is added to ice to change it into water. Although heat energy is still going into the material, there is no temperature change in the material, but a change in state. This energy is known as **latent heat**.

All of these energy levels can be described in terms of the movements of the molecules within the material (see Figures 2 to 4). The higher the energy level, the greater the movement of the molecules. So when steam is heated still further, it moves around so much (with so much energy) that it can exert pressure on its surroundings – this is particularly useful if the surroundings happen to be the piston of a steam engine.

Boiling and evaporating

The change from liquid to gas (or vapour) can occur by one of two processes.

Boiling is a process in which energy (heat) is added to a liquid to the point where it begins to change into a gaseous state. Molecules within the liquid now have sufficient energy to break free of the confines of the liquid. This change of state from liquid to gas usually takes place within the liquid nearest the source of the heat, causing bubbles of the gaseous form of the material to form within the liquid state. When the change from liquid to gas takes place, the energy goes into this change, rather than causing an increase in temperature.

Evaporation occurs at temperatures below the boiling point of the liquid. Rather than relying on extra energy to be put into the liquid to cause the change, molecules near the surface of the liquid take energy from neighbouring molecules to enable them to go through the change to a gas. Since the energy has been taken from the surrounding molecules, this has the effect of cooling them. Rain puddles dissipate because the water is evaporating into the surrounding air.

Condensing

As gaseous molecules lose energy to their environment (that is, they cool down), they go through the reverse of the evaporation process. Molecules now begin to form small droplets, usually on a surface that offers a particularly large energy (or more commonly, temperature) differential. On cold mornings the formation of dew, or even frost, on the ground from water vapour in the air is caused by the moisture in the air losing sufficient energy to change from a vapour to a liquid or even a solid (frost) state. In movement terms, the molecules of the gas will have slowed sufficiently for them to begin to collect together and form visible droplets of liquid matter.

Melting

The increase in the level of energy available to a solid (the warmer it gets!) the more that the molecules, which are held in a fixed arrangement, will move, or perhaps more accurately, vibrate. There will come a point, known as the **melting point**, where these molecules vibrate so much that they break out of the fixed arrangement and begin to flow. This is the point where extra energy will not increase the temperature of the material but will allow it to change state – from solid to liquid. Only when most of it has changed to liquid will any further increase in energy begin to lead to an increase in temperature. In effect, the increase in energy allows the individual molecules to break their attractive bond with adjacent molecules.

Freezing

As a liquid loses energy to its surroundings the molecules that make it up begin to move with less energy, more slowly. At this stage the reduction in energy levels does not lead to a further fall in temperature but the formation of bonds between molecules as they begin to form a regular structure. Attractive forces hold the molecules in a regular pattern, and only when the majority of the molecules are part of this structure does the temperature begin to fall further.

The whole process is reversible and can be repeated indefinitely as energy levels fluctuate. Figure 5 shows the various stages of the molecular movement in diagrammatic form.

Figure 5

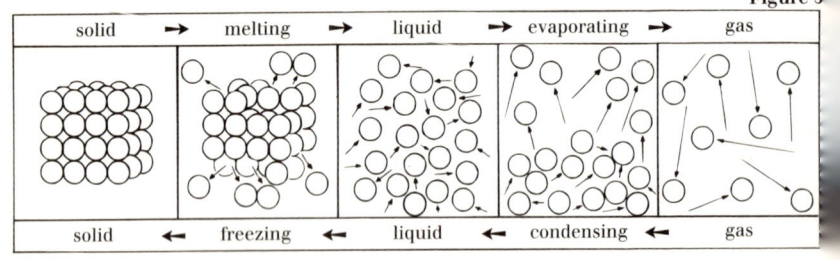

| solid | → | melting | → | liquid | → | evaporating | → | gas |
| solid | ← | freezing | ← | liquid | ← | condensing | ← | gas |

Pressure

As well as energy (or temperature), pressure has a role to play in the changes of state of a material. If the surrounding forces (pressure) are quite low, the material will be able to move from solid to liquid to gas at lower energy levels. Practically speaking, at very high altitudes water will begin to boil at a lower temperature – and consequently you will not be able to get a decent cup of tea in Nepal! If the pressure is increased, the changes from solid to liquid to gas will require more energy (a higher temperature) to take place – that's why a pressure cooker cooks food more quickly. In the case of boiling, the extra pressure means that a molecule (of water, say) will require more energy (more heat or a faster speed) before it is able to 'break free' of the mass of liquid. In the pressure cooker, more energy can be transferred from the water to the food, rather than being used by the water to change state (turn to steam). Gases such as propane and butane (the gases in gas cylinders) have to be kept at considerable pressure to keep them liquid at ambient temperatures (5°C to 20°C). Of the two cylinder gases used by campers and caravanners, butane is the most common, but since it liquefies at a higher temperature than propane, propane has to be used at lower temperatures.

As the molecules in a gas gain more energy (it gets hotter) they move around more and faster. If the gas is in an enclosed container it will exert more pressure on the internal surface. As they move faster they 'strike' the internal surface harder, causing more pressure. Either a more energetic (hotter) gas (see Figure 6) needs more space to be contained in (at the same pressure) or it will have to be held at a greater pressure (in the same space).

Expansion and contraction

As molecules begin to move around more (as they change from solid to liquid to gas) they need more space. In a solid the molecules will be bonded together quite closely; in a liquid they will have the space to move around each other; and in a gas they will move very much independently. This need for greater space will result in an expansion of the material. For a given amount of the material, in terms of the

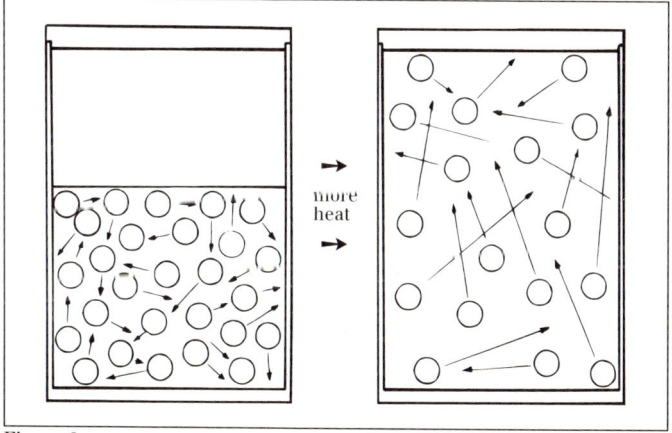

more heat

Figure 6

matter contained in it, it will take up an increasing volume as it changes from solid to liquid to gas.

Ice and water

The most common example of a material that goes through all three states of matter at reasonably attainable temperatures is water. The international system of measuring temperature is based on the behaviour of water – it freezes at 0ºC and boils at 100ºC. However, it is one of the few materials that goes against the rules: it expands as it turns to ice. This is actually amazingly fortuitous. The fact that this means that ice floats may not appear particularly important but is probably one of the key reasons why life is able to exist on Earth. The expansion of ice is one of the main forces that turns rock into smaller particles and finally soil (see Chapter 6, 'Changing Earth'). Since ice is less dense than water, it forms on the surface of water, not on the bottom. This is significant because it enables organisms to hibernate in the mud at the bottom of ponds, free from the fear of being frozen. As the coldest bit of water (the ice) is on the top, it easily receives energy from the Sun to turn it back to water.

If ice were to be more dense than water, it would sink and form on the bottom, far from the influence of the Sun, and so form a layer of permanent ice in the oceans. This layer would restrict the amount of ocean available to marine organisms and significantly limit the diversity of life in the oceans. In all probability, the vast proportion of the Earth's water would be locked up as deep sea ice, resulting in the majority of oceans being only a few tens of metres deep. At a more practical level, you will find that if you fill an ice cube tray to the very top and freeze it, the ice will rise up beyond the original water level. In the same way that ice can force apart rocks and lumps of soil, it can also achieve something similar with water pipes. If the water in metal pipes freezes, the force of the water expanding will split open the pipe – not too much of a problem until it melts and the water comes spurting out of the holes!

Subject facts

The change from solid to liquid to gas (and back) is one that children are aware of, though they do not necessarily appreciate its significance, as in the case of water. Developing a working understanding of the processes involved in moving from one state to another will provide a good foundation for a deeper understanding of the model suggested by the kinetic theory of matter.

Boiling – the process by which molecules in a liquid change into a vapour (much faster change than evaporation).
Condensing – the change of a vapour into a liquid, giving out energy as it changes.
Evaporation – the process by which molecules on the surface of a liquid change into a vapour.
Freezing – the change of a liquid to a solid, giving out energy as it changes.
Latent heat – the energy change in a material that leads to a change of state rather than temperature.
Melting point – the point at which a solid substance liquefies.
Vapour – the gaseous form of a material more commonly found in a liquid or solid form. A vapour is different from a gas in that a change of state can come about by changes in pressure alone, unaided by changes in temperature.

● Tungsten melts at 3420°C and finally boils at 5860°C.
● Helium stays as a gas down to –269°C and can't be turned into a solid at normal atmospheric pressure. Hydrogen can't even be turned into a liquid!
● The greatest rate of thermal expansion in a metal is shown by caesium, which expands at the rate of 0.0094% per °C.

Boiling and evaporation are the same thing.
The outcome is the same: a liquid becomes a vapour. However, there are significant differences. In both cases there is a need for the molecules to gain energy to change from the liquid to gaseous state. With evaporation, this energy is gained from the surroundings, thus cooling the surroundings down (that's why we perspire – the evaporation of the sweat takes heat from out bodies). Only those molecules on the surface are able to evaporate.
Boiling requires energy to be added (usually as heat), so as a liquid comes to the boil the temperature doesn't rise any further because the energy is being used to change the liquid into a gas. This process is faster than evaporation and occurs nearer the heat source rather than at the surface.

Steam is white.
Steam is actually clear (invisible) and dry. As water boils, some liquid particles of water are taken with the steam as it rises. As the steam begins to cool and **condense** back into

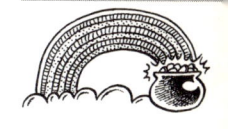

water, these droplets also become visible. The white 'cloud' that you can see coming from a boiling kettle of water is not steam or water vapour but very small droplets of water rising with the steam.

Why do air bubbles form in boiling water?
In fact, air bubbles don't, but steam bubbles do. As the water boils, it changes from liquid to a vapour (gas), and this happens nearest the source of the heat, usually at or near the bottom of the pan or kettle. As the steam is less dense than water the steam bubbles rapidly rise to the surface. These bubbles popping at the surface are what you see.

Why does water expand when it freezes into ice?
To be honest, this has always annoyed me as a teacher. It is the most obvious example that you can get to exemplify the changing states of matter – but then it doesn't do what it's supposed to but actually expands as it freezes! When water changes from liquid to solid at around 0°C it takes on a crystalline structure which arranges the H_2O (water) molecules in such a way that they take up more space than free flowing water. The formation of these hexagonal crystals means that the ice expands over the volume of water at the same temperature. It also means that it is less dense than water – ice floats on water.

Why do packets of frozen food go frosty on the outside when you bring them into the warmth of the kitchen?
This is really two questions. First, the obvious one of why does it happen, and second, the follow-up of where does the water for the frost come from? Frozen things tend to be very cold (well, that's made buying this book worthwhile!), at least colder than the ambient temperature of the kitchen. The frozen food will begin to warm, taking heat from the local environment to do so. Some of the immediate surroundings will give up so much of their heat energy that the temperature will drop to the freezing point of water. But where does this water come from? There is moisture in the air – sometimes this becomes visible when you breathe out on a cold day, but the moisture is always in your breath, even when you can't see it. There are many other ways that water vapour gets into the air – for example, from plants or the evaporation of puddles. The packet of frozen food is so cold that not only does it take enough energy from the water vapour in the air to make it condense, it also makes it freeze! And that's where the frost comes from.

Why does boiling water scald?

There is a considerable amount of energy locked up in boiling water as heat. When this comes into contact with skin there is an energy transfer from the water to the skin. Skin is a good heat insulator, which is a very useful property most of the time, but here that means that the energy cannot be spread out very easily so all the energy is absorbed locally. This overloads and damages the skin – it scalds it. Spraying or pouring cold water over the affected area dissipates the energy and reduces the damage if it is done quickly enough.

Changing state (recording)

Brainstorm with a group or class of children all of the materials that they know that change from solid to liquid or liquid to gas as they are heated. Record as pictures or a list.

Teaching ideas

Ice balloons (observing, recording)

Orinary ice cubes tend to melt too quickly to observe over a period of time, but a frozen water-filled balloon will last all day in most classroom conditions. Simply fill a balloon from a tap, knot the end and pop it in the freezer overnight – it shouldn't be too difficult to provide an ice balloon per group. Discuss what they are and how they were made. If ice has formed on the outside of the balloon, talk about this. Take the balloon off – if it isn't already ripped – to reveal the ice. Talk about its clarity (ice made from cooled, boiled water will be clearer with fewer impurities) and texture. Discuss where it might be kept to melt more quickly or slowly. Note when the water appears.

Note that the ice balloons are preferable because ice cubes of the same mass will melt more quickly. This is due to the increased surface area often giving insufficient time to get the ice cubes from the freezer and introduced to the session before they have melted.

Boiling (observing, recording)

As a demonstration, using a hot plate and a Pyrex saucepan, heat ice cubes until they melt and eventually boil them. Discuss the changes with the children as they occur. In particular, note the falling water level and the bubbles as the water begins to boil. Explain that the bubbles are filled with steam, not air – think about it: how can air suddenly appear in the water in bubbles? Ask the children to produce drawings to show the different stages that the ice cubes went through.

Melting and solidifying (observing, recording)
Many solids can be melted into liquids – brainstorm a few in the context of cooking (for example, fats – butter, margarine; chocolate; ice cream). Demonstrate a few examples to small groups using appropriate heat sources (see *Be Safe!* from the Association for Science Education, for details). A good example, other than those above, is offered by candles or night lights (they change from solid to liquid and then combustion can take place, though they can be heated to a gas without burning if no direct flame is used). Most other substances melt at too high a temperature for this activity to be safely managed in primary school. Others, such as most plastics, produce toxic fumes as they melt.

Condensing (observing, inferring)
As a demonstration, have a group of children observe a glass filled with a cold drink (add ice cubes if need be). Ensure that the outside of the glass is dry to begin with. Note the appearance of water droplets on the outside. Discuss with the children where these came from. (Water vapour in the air is condensing against the cold glass.)

Resources

Fridge/freezer
Heat source – kettle or hot plate
Balloons, plastic syringes
Pyrex saucepan
Examples (packaging or pictures) of solids, liquids and gases

Reference sources
Multimedia CD-ROM encyclopaedia (such as *Encarta*)
Dorling Kindersley *Science Encyclopedia*
Association for Science Education *Be Safe!*

Chapter 4
MIXING AND SEPARATING

Although the act of mixing and separating substances does not appear in the National Curriculum until KS2, much of what the children experience revolves around this – cooking, playing in sand and water, making orange squash and so on. Even if at R and KS1 this is seen as 'play', teachers need to be aware of what they are preparing the children for. The key ideas to be developed here are that:
1. There are different types of mixes.
2. Mixtures can be separated using various physical processes.
3. Physical changes can be modelled to explain the processes.
4. As substances are mixed or separated, their properties can change.

Mixing and separating concept chain
See 'The nature of "stuff" concept chain' on page 12 for general comments.

KS1
● Some substances (such as sand and water) can be mixed to achieve particular properties.
● Mixtures containing solid particles of different sizes (sand and beads) can be separated using a sieve.

KS2

● Some solids dissolve in water (soluble), some others do not (insoluble).
● Solutions can be separated by evaporation or distillation.
● Insoluble mixtures (suspensions) can be separated by filtration.
● For any soluble solid there is a maximum amount that can be dissolved in a given amount of water at a particular temperature.
● Liquids can be combined to form different types of mixtures.
● Substances are mixed to produce particular properties.

KS3

● Gases (such as air) can be mixed with a liquid to form a foam or with a solid to form a sponge.
● Liquids can mix to form an emulsion (such as salad cream – vinegar and vegetable oil).
● A **colloid** is a mixture of particles held in suspension, such as a solid (smoke) or liquid (hair spray) in a gas (air).
● All mixtures are a physical combination of substances and can be separated by physical means.
● The properties of a mixture may be very different from their components (such as a gel formed by combining gelatine powder and water).

Concept 1: Different types of mixes

Subject facts

Mixing substances

Substances can be combined in a number of ways. An important distinction to make is between the different levels on which this mixing takes place. At one level the different substances keep their original characteristics but they just happen to occupy much of the same space at the same time. These combinations can usually be separated out again quite easily. This sort of change is usually referred to as a **physical** or 'reversible' change and will be the focus of this chapter.

On another level, the chemical elements contained within the substances may react with each other and reconnect in different ways by forming new bonds. When substances combine in this way it is known as a **chemical** or 'irreversible' change (sometimes the change can be reversed, but it will usually be difficult or take considerable energy, or both). This type of change will be examined further in Chapter 5, 'Chemical changes'.

Basic mixes

You have to recognise that we are dealing with particles here. They can be of different sizes, I grant you, but we are definitely dealing with bits of different materials that can intermingle in different ways. Let's face it, by anybody's standards a ten-tonne slab of granite laid on top of a ten-tonne block of steel is not a mixture!

So what defines a 'mixture'? Think of it this way, wherever you take a small sample of a mixture you should be able to get, near enough, the same proportions of the substances that have been combined to make up the mixture. You should be able to allow for small fluctuations in the proportions, but a layer of one substance and a layer of another does not a mixture make!

So what's a mixture? There are plenty around. Soil is an example of different particles combining to make a mixture (see Chapter 6, 'Changing Earth'). My youngest son's bedroom floor is a mixture – of different types of Lego bricks, mainly! Young children just starting out in their formal education will usually not take long to start experimenting with mixtures by combining the contents of the water and sand trays and discovering that the new material they have produced has different properties from either of the constituent parts. They will quickly discover that there is a particular range of proportions in a mix of sand and water that allow the new material to be shaped and to retain its shape. They will discover that it is possible to have too much sand with the water (only parts of it seem to mix – much of the sand stays dry), or too much water with the sand (the sand just descends to the bottom of the pool). This is all part of learning that the proportions in the mixture are important, and that using different proportions will often result in the new material having different characteristics.

Particle size

Mixing particles of different sizes does have a significant effect on the resultant quantity of the mixture that is produced. Mixing one litre of dry sand with the same quantity of water or marbles will not produce two litres of the mixture. There is conservation of mass (the mixture will have the same mass as the two substances did individually) but not conservation of volume. This is because the particles have gaps between them which can be filled by smaller particles. The sand can fill the gaps between the marbles, and the water can fill the gaps between either the marbles or the grains of sand.

Types of mixture

The different types of mixture can be categorised according to the state of the different materials involved.

Solid in solid	Particulate mixture, alloy
Solid in gas	Smoke, dust suspension
Solid, liquid or gas in liquid	Suspension, solution
Liquid in gas	Aerosol
Liquid in liquid	Emulsion (a liquid in liquid suspension)
Liquid in solid (particulate or porous)	Absorption
Gas in solid	Sponge
Gas in liquid	Foam, solution

Colloids

The generic term for a mixture where particles of one type are temporarily held in place by particles of the other is a colloid. As far as the table above is concerned, all of the types described are colloids except for solid in solid, solutions, sponges and absorption because these can be maintained indefinitely, unless something else acts to change the mixture. In one way or another a colloid is a temporary to long-term suspension of one material in another. Temporary to long term? Well, suspensions can be very short term: stir or shake a spoon full of sand in a jar of water and the sand particles will whirl around in the water for a few moments to become a colloid before settling to the bottom. Smoke particles can hang around in the air as a colloid for very long periods (because they are so small). Usually they stay until they connect up with particles of moisture in the air and become massive enough to fall back to earth (or you walk into a room and inhale the particles of smoke).

Some particular types of colloid suspension are quite interesting – either in the way that they are formed or because of the materials that went into making them. Oil and water, you are often told, do not mix. You can even prove this to yourself by pouring some cooking oil into a half glass of water – it just floats on top. If you try stirring it, it mixes a bit but quickly separates out into two layers again. Adding it drop by drop and whipping it at the same time will blend the mixture into an emulsion – which will usually separate out in minutes rather than seconds. Commercially produced salad creams and mayonnaise will usually contain an 'emulsifying agent', which will help to keep the particles of oil in suspension for months. Another emulsion is milk – fat in water. The fat stays suspended for some considerable time, though if you do leave it long enough (and I'm sure that you've already carried out this experiment for yourself!) it will separate out.

Aerosol cans or diffusers (Figure 1) can be used to create a fine spray of liquid particles in a gas. These particles of liquid are so small that they can remain suspended in the air for considerable periods of time. Not only can such liquid delivery systems produce a fine spray, they can also produce a foam. Although you can mix air into cream to give it a light, fluffy texture (foam) it is also possible to get it in a can that produces ready whipped cream at the press of a button. If left long enough, the air will separate from the foam to leave the liquid cream (or at least what was once cream).

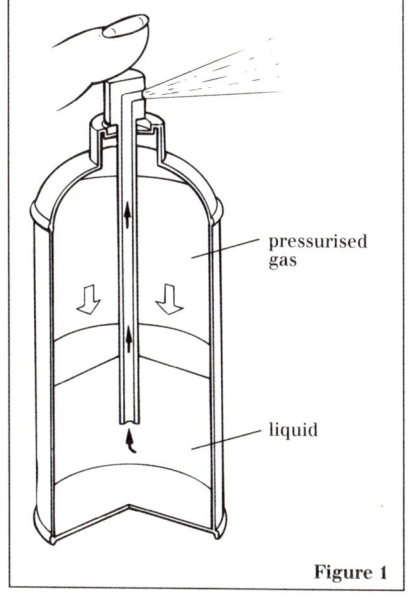

pressurised gas

liquid

Figure 1

Liquids and gases in solids

Solids, because of their very nature, do not flow or move around. In this respect they cannot suspend other particles in the same way that liquids and gases do. The gaps between the solid particles offer a space to be filled by even smaller particles, usually liquids and gases or other smaller solid particles. Solids can also take up structures that have internal spaces, such as foam rubber or Victoria sponge cake, or disposable nappies. While the spaces in the foam rubber are usually not connected, those in the cake and nappy are, allowing the air in them to be displaced by liquid. Dunking sponge cake in various types of alcoholic liquids is (not!) a matter to be trifled with. Basically, the absorbency of a material is dependent upon how much space within the structure can be filled with liquid. Try experimenting with the water retention qualities of different grades of sponge to prove this.

Dissolving

When a **solute** (the material that is going to dissolve) like salt, is placed in a **solvent** (the material that it is going to dissolve in) like water, the solute breaks down into its smallest salt components – salt molecules. What the solvent does is to break the bonds between the particles of the solute (should any exist) so that it becomes dispersed within the solvent. The difference between a **solution** and a colloid or **suspension** is that although they both have an even distribution of the material, a solution will have these particles at a molecular level, whereas for the colloid they will just be very small.

Different solvents can be used to dissolve different solutes. Water will dissolve sugar, but it won't do much good on greasy hands – you will need to apply a detergent or soap to dissolve grease. This is a surprisingly difficult concept for children to accept. Detergents, developed during the First World War by German scientists, are quite clever little molecules. They have a salt-based head, which is attracted to water (by the same forces that dissolve salt in water), and a long hydrocarbon 'tail', which forms a solution with the grease that sticks the dirt to the fabric (see Figure 2). In effect, the detergent molecule drags the dirt attached to the grease from the fabric into the water, allowing the water and grease (oil) to mix – hence dirty water.

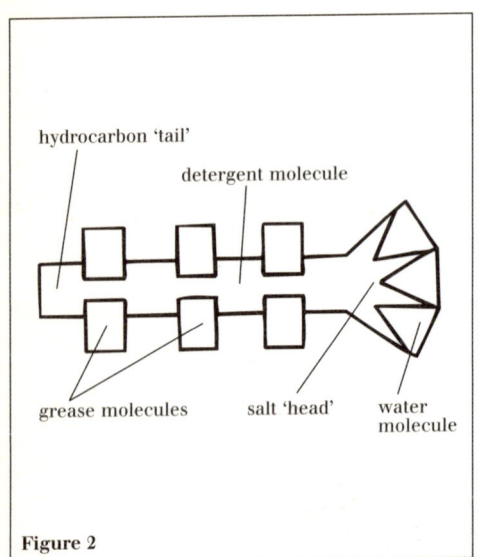

hydrocarbon 'tail'

detergent molecule

grease molecules salt 'head' water molecule

Figure 2

Most oil-based paints, such as household gloss paint, will only dissolve in a liquid such as oil of turpentine or white spirit – that's why you need to use one of those to clean your brushes. This leaves you with a brush covered in an oil-based product, which won't wash off with water, so you need another solvent, soap, to dissolve the paint cleaner. This is the same process that sea birds and marine mammals caught up in oil slicks have to go through. However, these creatures need a certain amount of oil in their coats (particularly feathers) to keep them water resistant. Stripped of their natural oils, feathers will absorb water.

As well as solids and liquids, gases can also be dissolved in liquid. When you look into a sealed bottle of carbonated lemonade, it appears little different from a bottle of water. It is only when the bottle top is undone that the gas dissolved in the lemonade makes itself known. To be contained within the restricted volume of the bottle, the gas is forced to dissolve – to find spaces between the molecules of liquid. When the bottle is opened, the pressure is released and some of the gas will take that opportunity to come out of solution – fizz! The dissolved carbon dioxide gas continues to be released from the liquid even after it has been drunk.

An interesting variety of a solution is a solid in solid (or more accurately, metal in metal) alloy. Examples of these solutions include brass (copper and zinc) and bronze (copper and tin). Although they end up as solids, they enter the solution as liquids – this is the only way that a uniform mix is possible at an atomic level – before cooling.

To sum up so far – some substances will dissolve, others will not. Of those materials that will dissolve, some will do so in water, others will only dissolve in different liquids. Some materials, such as metals, need to be melted before they will dissolve in each other.

Solubility

The rate at which a soluble substance will dissolve in a solvent is dependent upon a few key factors:

1. *The size of the particles.* The solvent acts on the surface area, so large sugar crystals will dissolve more slowly than granulated, which in turn will be slower than caster.

2. *The temperature of the solvent.* The hotter the tea, the more quickly the sugar dissolves, also the more sugar that can be dissolved – up to a point of 'super saturation' where no more solute can be dissolved unless there is an increase in the amount of solvent.

3. *The volume of solvent.* The bigger the cup of tea (of the same temperature as above), the more sugar that can be dissolved in it, again, up to the super saturation point for any given volume.

4. *The amount of stirring.* Being hotter just means that the solvent contains more energy (the molecules are moving about faster). It is the rise in energy level that causes the dissolving process to speed up. You can add energy to the system by giving the solution a good stir, imparting kinetic energy to it.

Mixing and separating

Why you need to know these facts

Some combinations of substances mix together more completely than others. Being able to identify and explain the differences is important both for classifying substances or processes and for identifying the potential methods of separation.

Vocabulary

Chemical change – one where the molecular structures of the combined substances are broken down and recombined to form new substances, making separation impossible (or nearly so).

Colloid – a suspension of small particles of one substance within another.

Physical change – one where the molecular structures of the combined substances stay separate, allowing separation to take place.

Solute – the substance that is dissolved.

Solution – the dispersion, at a molecular level, of one substance within another.

Solvent – what the material is dissolved in.

Suspension – a substance that contains small particles of another substance floating around in it.

Amazing facts

● The 30 000 tonnes of oil spilled from the tanker Exxon *Valdez* in 1989 was spread along 2400km of the coastline of Alaska. Fortunately, less coastal damage was caused when in 1979 the Atlantic *Empress* deposited 287 000 tonnes of oil in the Caribbean when it collided with another ship.

Common misconceptions

Sugar disappears when it is mixed into water.
Teachers often regard this use of the word 'disappeared' as a simple misconception. Before jumping on a child and saying, 'No, you're wrong! It dissolves!', ask them what they mean. If they are using 'disappeared' in the sense that they can no longer see it, then it's hard to argue with them and certainly confusing to say that they are wrong. If they mean that the sugar has 'gone', ask them if they can tell a glass of pure water apart from a glass of sugary water. If they say that they can if they taste the water, then they clearly recognise that the sugar has not 'gone' and is still there. They should be encouraged to use the word 'dissolved' as a fuller, more accurate description of what has happened.

POCKET GUIDES: MATERIALS

Why does dissolved icing sugar turn the water white?
Icing sugar looks like any other refined sugar – that is, white. Apart from the size of the particles it looks no different from granulated or caster sugar – but it is. It contains a white colouring agent. Why? When you mix icing, what colour is it? White, right? If it dissolved like any other sugar it would be clear – who wants see-through icing on a cake?

Why do sugar lumps dissolve so fast if it is all about surface area?
It *is* about surface area. Sugar lumps aren't solid, they are separate granules pressed together. The tea gets in and breaks the granules up, giving it more surface area to work on.

Questions

Soluble? (testing, sorting)
Use small, clear plastic containers, water and a range of powders and granules (such as sand, flour, salt, sugar, instant coffee and chalk). The children work in small groups to design a fair test to see which of the substances dissolve in water, which are colloids and which don't mix. Children should be encouraged to explain how they did each test, and they should record their results systematically in a table.

How soluble? (testing, predicting, recording)
Using a substance that will dissolve (best to stick with salt or sugar), brainstorm the factors that might affect the rate of dissolving with the class. Factors should include the amount of water, the temperature of the water, the stirring action, the amount of solute and the size of solute particles. As a class, predict and record. Small groups take one of these factors each and plan and carry out a fair test. Each group presents its findings to the class. Do not use boiling water – water from a hot tap will be sufficient.

Chromatography (testing, recording)
Using water-based felt pens and blotting (or better still filter) paper, children choose a pen and make a mark in the middle of the filter paper (see Figure 3). They then drip water on to the dot to make it blot. As the ink runs, the different colours that have been used to make the ink will spread out by differing amounts to give different coloured patterns. Are all black pens made from the same colours? Do all inks blot with water?

Teaching ideas

Catering mix (testing, observing)

Cooking starts with mixing – that is, mixing ingredients to obtain different tastes and textures and colours and smells and… I think you get the point. So with small groups of children carry out some basic culinary activities: mix up a breakfast muesli, a jelly, a cordial. Beat an egg, whip cream, dunk a biscuit! Try making different recipes that don't require heating to bring about a change. As you do so, talk to the children about what is happening to the mixtures.

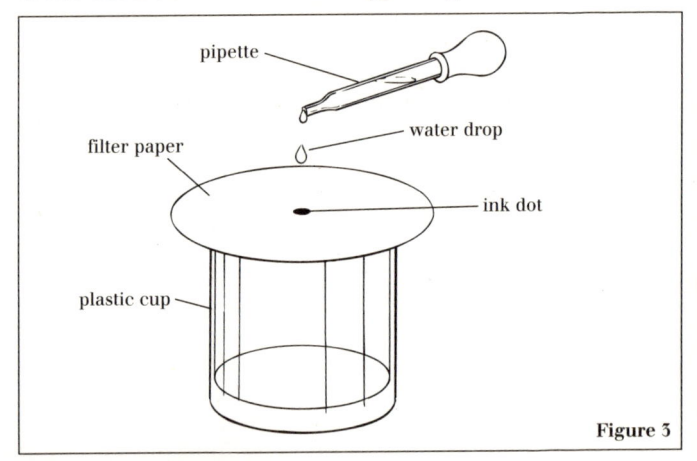

Figure 3

Concept 2: Separating mixtures

Subject facts

Okay, so you've made your mixture, now what do you want to do? Separate it out, of course! The way you do this will depend upon the nature of your mixture and which part of the mixture you want to collect.

Some mixtures that are not **miscible** (that is, mixtures that don't mix – colloids, after the larger particles have settled to the bottom), often solid–liquid or liquid–liquid combinations, can be separated by skimming. As they don't mix, they will form different layers that can be separated

Figure 4

from each other. Skimmed milk (surprisingly enough) is an example of this (see Figure 4). The cream forms a layer over the milk and can be (wait for it!) skimmed off! And semi-skimmed milk has only some of the cream skimmed off. The same happens with oil and water.

Immiscible solids in a liquid (usually water) can be removed in much the same way. Sand or soil or talcum powder if shaken in water to form a temporary suspension, will eventually settle out to form sediment at the bottom on the liquid. In fact the soil and the talcum powder, as they frequently contain different sized particles, will sediment in different layers. Soil will form from the bottom up (as shown in Figure 5) as

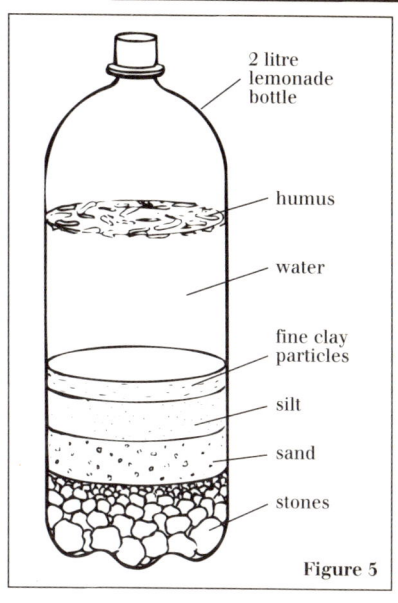

2 litre lemonade bottle

humus

water

fine clay particles

silt

sand

stones

Figure 5

progressively smaller particles, from large stones to fine particles of clay. The proportions of these different sized particles helps to classify soils. (See the teaching idea on **sedimentation** below.)

Filtration

Where there is a mixture of different sized particles – we are talking of some form of colloid or suspension here – a sieving or **filtration** system can be used to catch the larger particles. A mixture of sand and marbles or peas in the sand tray can easily be separated by using a sieve with holes large enough for the sand to go through but not the peas or marbles. Very similar processes are used for tea bags, cafetières and boiled potatoes – they all use some form of sieve which allows the water through but nothing else. The larger particles in dirty water can be extracted by passing it through a filtration system (similar to Figure 6) – but this does not make it safe to drink! You could try filtering cola in the same way and see what drips into the collecting cup at the bottom (this will give a few ideas about the size of the particles used for the colour).

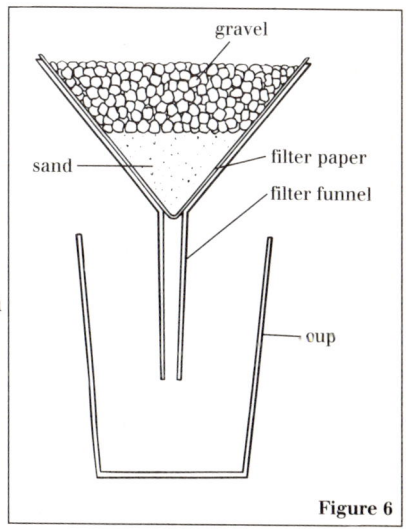

gravel

sand

filter paper

filter funnel

cup

Figure 6

Separating solutions

Because these are mixtures at the molecular level, sieves of an appropriate size are difficult to make. A special kind of filter or semi-permeable membrane can be used to separate a sugar solution. This membrane has microscopic holes that allow the water molecules through, but not the sugar molecules – it will work, but will be painfully slow. Plants and animals have quite well-developed membrane systems for extracting oxygen from air or water. The membrane allows oxygen to pass through, but prevents other gases or water getting in.

Separation processes for solutions tend to rely upon the different substances in the solutions having different boiling or evaporation points. Salt can be recovered from saline by allowing the water to evaporate. The level of alcohol in wine, say, can be reduced in a similar way (though this is not a very frequent occurrence!). There are also situations where a colloid will be separated by evaporation rather than filtration or sedimentation. Particles of clay are very small and will tend to stay in suspension for a long time. Being so small the clay particles will also block up filtration systems. By allowing the water to evaporate, the clay can be recovered much more effectively.

There are occasions where allowing one of the substances in the solution to evaporate will mean allowing the substance that you want retained being the one that you 'lose' (like the alcohol from the wine). In cases such as this, evaporation will still be the process used to separate the solution, but it will be combined with condensation. The part of the mixture that evaporates first will be collected and cooled, causing it to revert to a liquid state (condensed) so that it can be easily collected. This whole process is known as **distillation**.

Fresh water can be collected from saline using distillation in a desalination plant. Purer forms of alcohol can be extracted from alcohol solutions by distillation in a distillery. An oil refinery employs distillation to separate the lighter grades of oil, such as petrol, from the heavier elements, such as bitumen.

Why you need to know these facts

Much of chemistry revolves around separating substances from each other. The practical applications for the children are equally important, offering solutions to everyday problems. Children will have practical experience of learning through play with sand and water, and you can build on this experience.

Distillation – the collection of an evaporate by cooling.
Filtration – the collection of larger particles in a mixture.
Miscible – a mixable mixture (leading to an even distribution of the substance throughout).
Sedimentation – allowing suspended particles in a mixture to settle.

Vocabulary

● Crude oil is distilled many times, each at a slightly higher temperature to evaporate off increasingly dense oil-based products – petroleum, then aviation fuel, diesel and kerosene, fuel oils, lubricants, waxes (Vaseline), grease, bitumen, and asphalt. Separating a mixture into many different parts is known as fractional distillation.

Amazing facts

Filtered stream water is safe to drink.
Filtration does take the big lumps out of water, but there are many nasty things that are small enough to find their way through sand and even filter paper. Various micro-organisms and chemical compounds such as pesticides will still be present.

Common misconceptions

Why does flour mix with hot water but not cold water?
Flour is a quite complex organic substance that does not mix with water. When it is heated, as it is when mixed with hot water, a chemical change takes place allowing it to combine with water molecules in an irreversible change. So it doesn't mix like, say, salt. Chemical changes like this are described in Chapter 5, 'Chemical changes'.

Questions

Sieving (sorting, observing)
Using a collection of sieves, individuals or small groups of children can separate out a prepared mixture of dry, particulate materials (such as marbles, peas, rice, sand, flour – depending upon the sieves that you have available). The children will need to discuss the effectiveness of the process and suggest other situations where it might be employed.

Teaching ideas

Filtration (sorting, observing)
Ask a small group of children to construct a filtration device (see Figure 6 for ideas – the trick is to trap the larger particles) and then provide them with suspensions to

separate (water with rice, sand, flour, etc.). Which ones separate the quickest? Are there any where the separation does not appear to be complete? Are there particles that are small enough to get through? Examine what has been retained in the filter, and what has passed through. Ask the children to suggest where else this process might be used – for example, cleaning dirty water.

Sedimentation (observing)

Place a mixture of dry, insoluble particulate materials (such as a dried soil sample) into a plastic sweet jar (or lemonade bottle – though you will probably need to cut and reseal it). Add about twice the amount of water and shake until the particles are in suspension. Wait (and we may be talking days here) and observe what happens as it sediments out.

Evaporating (observing, recording)

Have groups of children make up strong salt solutions using a measured amount of salt. Discuss with the children the best conditions for evaporation to take place (warm, dry, large surface area of the liquid). Pour into uncovered containers and place them somewhere where they will not be disturbed over a period of several days. The children should return to them a couple of times per day (especially in warm weather or when the experiment is carried out in a warm area of the classroom) and record by drawings or photographs what is happening. When all of the water has evaporated, is the original quantity of salt left? Does it look the same as it did before it was dissolved?

Condensing (observing, recording, testing)

Prepare a salt solution as above in hygienic conditions. Have members of the group taste the solution to note the saltiness – only taste a drop on the tongue under hygienic conditions. Place the salt solution in a bowl on a tray under the top portion of a plastic lemonade bottle (see Figure 8).

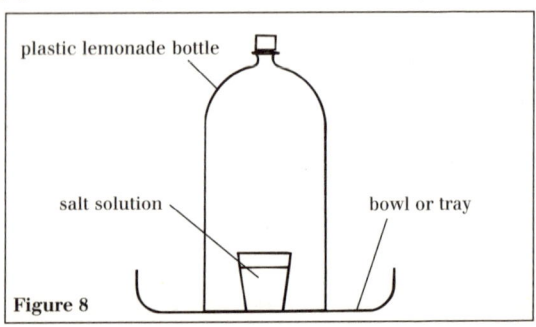

plastic lemonade bottle

salt solution

bowl or tray

Figure 8

Ensure that all of the equipment is hygienically clean. Encourage the children to observe the water droplets forming on the inside of the bottle and the fall in the level of water in the cup. Tap the bottle to make the droplets run down. The water in the bowl should be safe to taste – is the saltiness still there?

Concept 3: Modelling mixtures

Suspensions

Where one substance is held suspended in another, the differences in the sizes of the particles is quite significant. Generally the particles of the substance that are in suspension are significantly larger – particles of smoke can be seen, particles of air cannot. So how are the bigger bits held in suspension? Mainly by the movements of all of the small particles around them. Think about it. You can keep a balloon, or maybe even a table tennis ball suspended in the air by blowing on it. For as long as you can keep a stream of fast moving air molecules coming out of your mouth you can counteract the pull of gravity. This is basically what happens to keep small particles of smoke in the air, or talcum powder in water (see Figure 9). This is why, when you stir up muddy or sandy water, the particles become suspended rather than lying at the bottom as sediment. Making the water move more allows it to pick up or suspend more or bigger particles – that's why there is more dust flying around in the air on windy days.

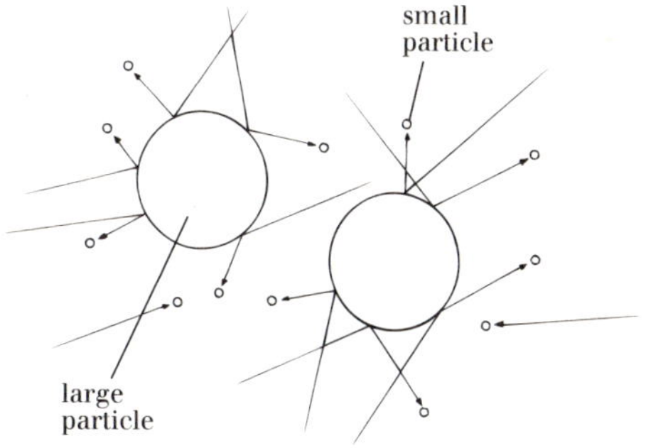

As there is such a great difference in size between the particles, sieving or filtration can separate the two substances (see Figure 10).

Figure 9

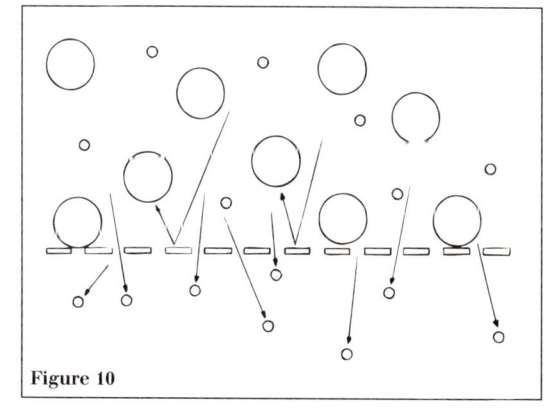

Figure 10

The greater the difference in size, the easier this filtration process is as the hole can be made large enough to allow the smaller particles to go through very quickly.

Solutions

As this is a mixture at a molecular level the particles are of a much more similar size to each other. The solute will become evenly dispersed until it reaches a state of **saturation**. At this point, no more of the solute will dissolve without either the addition of more solvent or more heat.

A salt solution is an interesting one to model. Salt is an example of an ionically bonded structure (of sodium and chlorine) and water is an example of covalent bonding (see Chapter 1 for more details). When the salt crystals enter the water, the water molecules start to get between the ions (atoms that have too many or too few electrons attached to them as a result of bonding). In the covalent bonded water molecule an atom of oxygen shares the electrons of two hydrogen atoms. Although this does not mean that they have particularly positive or negative charges, there is a tendency for the oxygen to be attracted to positively charged particles and the hydrogen in the bond to be attracted to negatively charged particles (see Figures 11a and b).

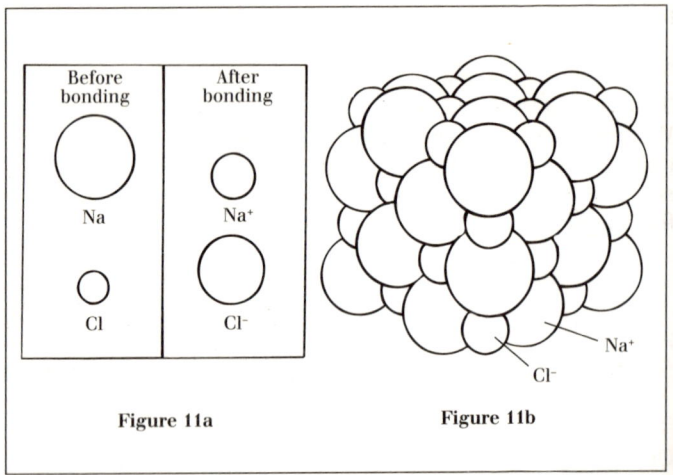

Before bonding	After bonding
Na	Na⁺
Cl	Cl⁻

Figure 11a

Figure 11b

The hydrogen 'end' of the water molecule is attracted to the chlorine ion and the oxygen to the sodium. The water forms a barrier between the ionically bonded salt ions causing the salt to break up – to dissolve. As the water in the solution evaporates, there is no longer enough to form a barrier between the sodium and chlorine ions so they once more begin to bond and form a crystalline structure.

Moving beyond what the children need to know for KS2, this section offers the teacher a visualisation of the processes involved in the mixing and separating of substances.

Why you need to know these facts

Saturation – point at which no more solute can be dissolved in solvent.

Vocabulary

Filter-tipped cigarettes are safer than those without.
Well, that's what the adverts claimed in the 1950s, but it has since been proved that it's the smaller particles in the smoke that do most of the damage. In any case, the companies ensured that the size of the filters allowed sufficient quantities of the carcinogenic substances through to give the 'taste'!

Common misconceptions

At what point does a suspension become a solution?
When the particles are of a molecular size and they are evenly distributed throughout the solute, then it is a solution. Furthermore, solutions cannot be separated by filtration.

Questions

Concept 4: New properties of a mixture

Subject facts

One of the key clues that give away the fact that you are now dealing with a mixture rather than a pure substance is the change in properties. Sand, when small amounts of water have been added, is capable of being moulded; water tastes different when sugar has been added, and copper is made stronger when it is alloyed with 10% tin to make bronze. By combining materials as mixtures it is possible to either change the properties or to improve certain desirable ones.

Fabric

Quite frequently fabrics are made from combinations of different materials (or, to avoid confusion, fibres). Different fibres have different qualities and by combining them in appropriate proportions particular qualities can be obtained. Cotton is strong and a good insulator and Lycra is very elastic, so a fabric that combines these properties should be hard wearing and warm to wear and will return to shape after stretching. Nylon, while strong, tough and elastic, does not 'feel' particularly appealing, but when it is mixed with wool it makes a very hard wearing and attractive carpet at a much lower cost than pure wool.

Soil

It may seem strange to think of soil as a mixture, but ask any good gardener about the properties of different soils! Figure 5 demonstrates how the different sized particles in soil can be separated out. Clay soils (very fine particles) do not drain well, sandy soils (coarse particles) drain far too well – neither are particularly wonderful as growing media. If these soils are mixed their productivity improves significantly as the mixture now retains the correct amount of water to support plant growth (though this does vary enormously). Adding substances such as compost or sand to a very heavy clay soil will improve the fertility.

Gel

Gel is a particular mixture of solid and liquid that produces another solid. Gelatine, made by boiling down animal bones, is a very brittle substance, but when it is dissolved in water the mixture becomes very elastic. The gelatine absorbs in the region of five times its own mass of water and forms complex connections, which gives the gel its solid shape.

Food preparation without cooking (so chemical changes are less likely) revolves round changing properties of food (textures and tastes) as ingredients are combined.

Why you need to know these facts

Often the reason why substances are mixed (or mixtures are separated) is because of the properties that they exhibit. Mixing substances to achieve the desired properties is something that children consider as soon as they start to mix sand and water to build a sandcastle.

Vocabulary

Gel – a particular mixture of solid and liquid that will produce another solid.

Amazing facts

● Gold fillings are only 58% gold – the rest is silver and copper.
● Stainless steel can be as little as 60% iron – the rest is nickel and chromium).

Common misconceptions

The oceans are so big that any pollution will just mix in.
Pollutants in the ocean do not necessarily disperse evenly. Some, such as oil, do not even dissolve. So while the *very* long-term effect may be only a minor change to the contents of the ocean, in the short term and in localised spots, the properties of the ocean may be changed significantly, making it impossible for the existing forms of life to survive. Some pollutants are so toxic that only a very small concentration can cause significant problems.

Questions

Why do gardeners add manure or compost to the soil?
Adding this organic matter will have different effects in different soils. In sandy soil (large particles) it will help to bind the soil together to retain moisture and nutrients. In a clay soil (very small particles) it will break it up, allowing moisture to drain and air to get into the soil for soil microbes to be more active and produce more plant nutrients.

Sandcastles (exploration testing)
In small groups children can try to discover the best mix of sand and water to make sandcastles. How can the different mixes be measured, recorded and tested?

Squash (testing, recording)
What's the best mix of squash and water? Have a group of children carry out a survey to discover the most popular proportions of cordial and water.

Teaching ideas

Mixed fibres (recording, comparing)
Make a collection of, say, shirts that are similar but made from fabrics with different fibre mixes. Record the fibres and the mixes. Compare their properties using samples cut from each.

Muesli mixtures (recording, comparing)
Collect different brands of muesli. Compare the contents – both the actual ingredients and the proportions. Compare them for price and other properties.

Resources

Plenty of 'safe' kitchen chemicals (powdered foodstuffs) for mixing
Other mixtures such as sands, soils and so on
Clear plastic pots and two-litre lemonade bottles for mixing
Various grades of sieves
Filter paper and funnels
A range of mixtures, including foodstuffs as examples and for separating

Chapter 5
CHEMICAL CHANGES

Key concepts

This goes beyond the simple mixing of substances to a point where the chemical components of the substances are deconstructed and then reconstructed to form new materials. Much of the construction of new materials here relates back to 'Molecular Models' on pages 18–21. The key ideas to be developed here are that:
1. Change can be described as either reversible or irreversible.
2. Chemical change can either use or release energy.

Chemical changes concept chain
See 'The nature of "stuff" concept chain' on page 12 for general comments.

KS1
● Some processes (such as cooking) lead to irreversible changes in the properties of the materials.
● Some substances can be heated and cooled (such as chocolate) and returned to their former condition but if heated more they change (burn) and cannot return to their former condition.
● Some changes (such as burning) can release heat.

KS2

● **Physical changes** (such as drying clay) can be reversed but **chemical changes** (such as firing clay) cannot.
● Some irreversible changes require heat (cooking, firing); others (burning) produce heat.
● The properties of a material that result from a chemical change are different from those of the original material.

KS3

● Chemical changes make new materials at the level of the bonds between atoms.
● Most chemical changes are difficult to reverse.
● In the making of new materials, energy is either required or released.

Concept 1: Chemical changes

Subject facts

Materials can experience two types of physical change: a change of state due to heating or cooling, and changes due to physical mixing or separating. Chemical changes take place on a molecular level, with molecular structures being rearranged to produce new materials. These new materials will contain all of the same elements as the old ones, but they will be significantly altered in their properties.

Chemical changes are the result of particular processes that, once complete, are often very difficult to reverse, unless by a different reaction. The carbon cycle is one that is based on biochemical processes. Carbon (see Figure 1) is extracted from the carbon dioxide in the atmosphere through a process called **photosynthesis**. The carbon is then combined with water to form various types of

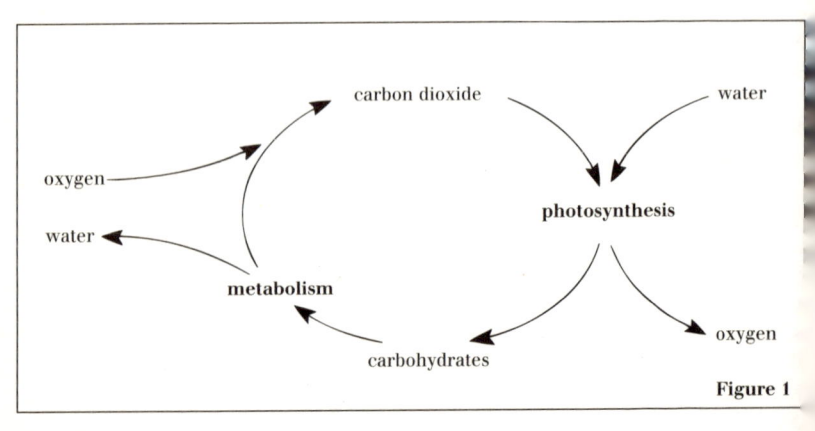

Figure 1

carbohydrate. With the addition of oxygen, organisms are able to metabolise the carbohydrate to release energy (and release carbon dioxide back into the atmosphere). Although the carbon is recycled, the processes are not reversed: photosynthesis and metabolism are one-way processes.

Heating will sometimes cause a chemical change to take place rather than a change of state. Chocolate, if warmed, will change from solid to liquid and will revert to solid when cooled. If it is heated further, a chemical reaction (burning) will take place from which it will not be able to return.

Another one-way change is from clay to ceramic. If clay is dried it will take on a pottery-like property – it will be brittle, not plastic. But if water is added, it can be remoulded. Once the pottery is fired, it has not only dried out but its chemical bonding has also altered so it will no longer revert to sticky clay if immersed in water – quite a useful property if you are carrying hot tea in it at the time!

Cooking provides familiar examples of chemical changes that the children can experience and explore. Food contains three main types of chemicals – proteins, carbohydrates and fats. Very little happens to fat when it is placed in boiling water but carbohydrates (such as potatoes and pasta) absorb water and soften for easier digestion. Protein-based food changes chemically on heating, identifiable in terms of taste, texture or appearance. Organic materials go through chemical changes that can be identified by taste among other senses. Cooking causes detectable chemical changes to occur. Once cooked, the humble carrot, crunchy and rigid in its raw state, assumes a significantly different structure. Even when cooled to its original temperature it still lacks the texture that it once possessed. A cooked carrot stays cooked. It is much the same with milk. It can be warmed, to some extent, and then cooled and still retain its original flavour. But once it is heated, particularly if it is boiled, it will change chemically so even if it is chilled, it will still taste different. This explains the difference between the flavours of pasteurised (72°C for 15 seconds) and 'long-life' milk (UHT or 'ultra-heat treatment' – heated to a temperature of over 100°C for a shorter period).

Another food-based reaction involves acid. Sherbet 'fizzes' on the tongue. This is because the moisture in your mouth allows a chemical reaction to take place. The active ingredients in sherbet are sodium bicarbonate and citric acid crystals (with icing sugar for taste!). Apart from the sodium, the only other elements involved are hydrogen, oxygen and carbon. When the acid and sodium bicarbonate come into contact in a wet environment (your mouth) a reaction takes place that produces a much greater volume of carbon dioxide than there was powder before (the mass is unchanged though). The reaction will only stop when one or the other of the **reactants** has been used up. Baking powder contains both sodium bicarbonate and a powdered acidic compound – so all you need to do is add water.

The decay of food is also the result of chemical change. Once the food is spoilt it cannot be returned to its original condition. These chemical changes take place as the result of the action of micro-organisms – bacteria and fungi. Although such changes cannot be reversed they can be slowed or prevented. The heat treatment of milk is an attempt to kill the organisms present in the milk to delay the onset of changes. The action of these microbes is dependent on several environmental factors within and surrounding the foodstuff. If these can be removed, the growth of the micro-organisms will be delayed or prevented. For growth these micro-organisms require oxygen, an appropriate temperature, water, and the absence of poisonous chemicals. Food preservation will clearly depend upon the removal of these factors by:

● vacuum packing (for example, coffee) or canning (vegetables) to remove the oxygen;
● freezing or refrigeration to prevent growth, or heating to kill the microbes prior to sterile packing;
● drying (fruits and fish);
● the use of chemicals such as acids (pickling), salt (meat and fish) and sugar (fruit, as in jam).

Radiation is also being used more frequently to kill microbes and increase the 'shelf life' of soft fruit.

There is a group of **anaerobic** microbes (ones that live in the absence of oxygen) called methanogen. These microbes live by metabolising hydrogen and carbon dioxide in decaying organic matter to form methane. They are specifically used in the final treatment of sewage to break down the 'sludge' and are also naturally found in the digestive tract, particularly of ruminants such as cattle.

The distinctions between chemical and physical changes (such as mixing) are sometimes very hard to determine by purely observational means. Just saying that chemical changes are irreversible and physical changes can be simply reversed using physical means is not always true. You can always find an exception – try making a jelly (gel) revert to water and gelatine! This provides another example of the rules of science not being 'hard and fast'. It is best to consider each example independently rather than to give over-simplistic definitions.

The difference between simply mixing different substances (a cake mix) and bringing about a non-reversible change in those substances to form a new material (cooking the cake) is one which most children are aware of but have not explored in any guided or detailed way.

Why you need to know these facts

Vocabulary

Anaerobic – respiration without the use of oxygen.
Chemical change – one where the molecular structures of the combined substances are broken down and recombined to make new substances.
Physical change – one where the molecular structures of the combined substances stay separate, allowing separation to take place.
Reactants – substances that react with one another chemically to form a new substance (or substances).

Amazing facts

● Canned food stored at an Antarctic research station remained edible for more than 50 years.
● Protein becomes tougher the more it is cooked – a ten minute boiled egg will be more or less indigestible.

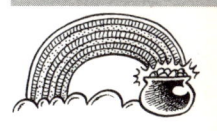

Common misconceptions

Chemical changes happen in factories.
Chemical changes happen all around us (and inside us). These changes were going on long before there were humans, let alone factories. Factories or chemical plants are used to make chemical processes more efficient or to produce larger quantities of the new materials.

Questions

How do I know that a chemical rather than physical change has taken place?
It is quite possible that you will not. Sometimes the differences are easier to identify than others. In some cases there will be an obvious change in properties that does not reverse, or a use or release of energy (mainly heat – that is, cooking or burning), but this it not always the case. It is often only by being told and building up a list of examples for comparison that a better understanding of the differences between physical and chemical changes is achieved.

Egg whites (observing, testing)

As a supervised activity, a small group of children using a Pyrex saucepan and a heat source can observe the changes in egg whites. Egg whites are about 9–10% protein and so will change when heated. This can be done in hot water. The children might like to test to see what temperature of water is required to make the transparent egg white become opaque.

Fizzy sherbet (observing, testing)

How much carbon dioxide is produced by a given amount of sherbet? Using a set-up similar to Figure 2, the children can carry out an investigation to find out. Does it depend upon the amount of water? The temperature of the water? If making your own sherbet, what are the most productive proportions of sodium bicarbonate and citric acid? How much gas does the same amount of baking powder produce?

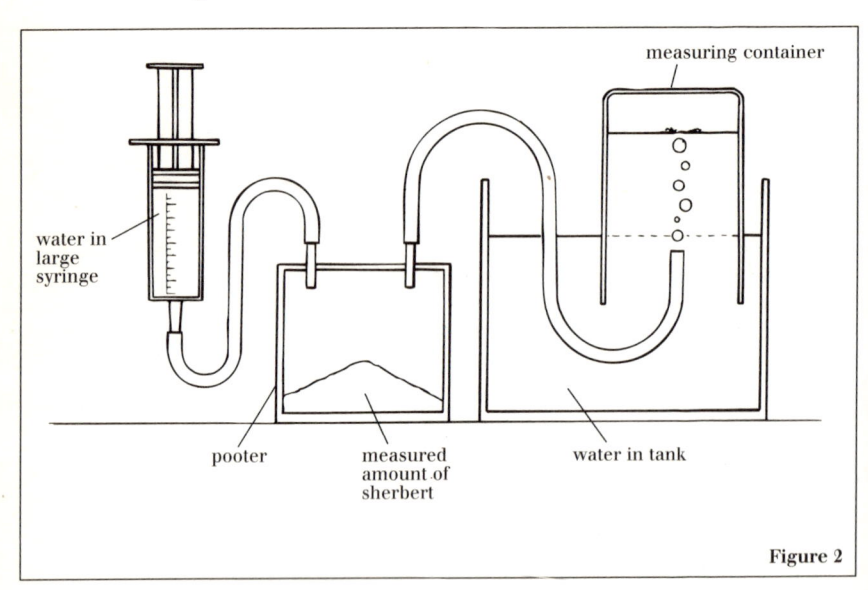

water in large syringe

measuring container

pooter

measured amount of sherbert

water in tank

Figure 2

Chemical/physical (observing and recording)

More advanced children may be able to begin to make lists of chemical and physical changes. By researching the processes (in, for example, *Children's Britannica, Encarta,* Dorling Kindersley's *Science Encyclopedia*) children can begin to record the chemical process taking place.

Concept 2: Making new materials

Not all chemical changes are announced by smells or explosions; nor are they the preserve of chemists with test tubes. These changes can be described in terms of the rearrangement of molecular bonds or the energy that is released or used in the process. The energy changes are particularly useful ones to explore. Where heat is required for the reaction to take place and continue (such as in cooking or firing) it is termed an **endothermic reaction**. An **exothermic reaction** (such as **combustion**) releases heat to the surroundings. This is not the production of 'new' energy, just the transfer of one form to another.

Some of the more interesting chemical changes involve reactions with oxygen. One, metabolism, has already been mentioned above; others include combustion and rusting (oxidisation of metallic materials). While photosynthesis requires energy (endothermic) from the Sun, metabolism releases energy (exothermic). When combustion of, for example, methane (CH_4) occurs, oxygen (O_2) reacts with it to form two new substances, carbon dioxide (CO_2) and water (H_2O). As this reaction takes place heat is produced. There is no change in the actual chemicals present, or their quantities, just a rearrangement of their bonds. It is quite interesting to note that two gases react to form another gas and a liquid – though the water does not appear as a liquid at the time of the reaction because of the heat involved. As the quantities will be the same before and after the reaction, an equation can be used to show the combustion:

$$CH_4 + 2O_2 \rightarrow CO_2 + 2(H_2O)$$
There have to be two lots of oxygen. In total there are four hydrogen and oxygen atoms and an atom of carbon.

There are two molecules of water for every one of carbon dioxide produced by the reaction. In total there are still four hydrogen and oxygen atoms and an atom of carbon. And there's heat as well! The heat is produced by the breakdown of the carbon/hydrogen bonds. The materials produced by the reaction are chemically simpler than the originals.

While this oxygen reaction is fast, other combustions can vary from the gentle warmth of a peat fire to the explosive qualities of hydrogen. It is interesting to note that if hydrogen were to be used as a combustion fuel rather than hydrocarbons (such as petrol and diesel) no waste carbon dioxide would be produced, leading to a 'cleaner' atmosphere. Just look at the reaction equation:

$$2H_2 + O_2 \rightarrow 2(H_2O) \qquad \textit{All you get is water and heat!}$$

When oxygen reacts with metal, the change may be fast or slow depending on the metal. Most metals tarnish in air due to the presence of oxygen, but caesium reacts so quickly it burns, producing heat and a bright light. Some, like gold, hardly react at all, while others, such as lead, react very quickly to form a surface barrier that prevents further reactions. One of the most common is the reaction of iron and oxygen to form iron oxide. Unlike copper and lead, where this oxidised layer protects the metal underneath, iron oxide also combines with water and expands. This causes it to flake off, allowing the air to come into contact with the iron underneath so that more iron becomes oxidised. This process is commonly called 'rusting'. The oxidised iron gives iron ore, rust and blood that red colour (in the body the red blood cells are the oxygen carriers).

Food chemical reactions
The use of a reactant, such as baking powder in cake making, will cause a selection of ingredients, when cooked, to adopt a firm but spongy texture. The proteins contained in the flour provide the firm structure while the carbon dioxide from the baking powder reaction provides the gas-filled pockets (the springiness). When making bread, yeast is used instead of the baking powder. The yeast, a type of fungi, uses the carbohydrate in the flour as a food source and produces carbon dioxide as a waste product. Various types of dairy produce also rely on chemical changes brought about by the action of micro-organisms.

Pasteurisation kills most of the bacteria present in milk, but not all of it. In any case, there are usually enough floating around in the atmosphere. If milk is left long enough, the remaining bacteria will become plentiful enough to have an appreciable effect on the structure of the milk. Lactose, a sugar present in the milk, will be used as a food source by the micro-organisms and turned into lactic acid. This will provide a 'tangy' taste – the first sign that milk is beginning to 'turn', to go sour. If enough of this acid is produced it will make the protein in the milk **coagulate**, that is 'clump together'. This change is known as curdling, as the milk is separated into curds (lumps) and whey (clear liquid). The curds can be fed to more bacteria to turn it into cheese, and it can then be infected with various moulds to add the 'veins' to cheeses like Stilton. Yoghurt is produced in a similar way, but the milk is not allowed to separate fully.

Plastics

There are many chemical reactions that are part of children's everyday experience, such as cooking and the life processes of metabolism and respiration. They are probably not aware of these in those terms. A large proportion of the materials that they will encounter are the product of either natural (as in the case of rocks and timber) or synthetic complex chemical reactions. The plastics industry is also based upon hydrocarbons. Rather than getting the hydrocarbons to combust and release energy by becoming simpler molecules, plastics are produced by combining simple molecules (**monomers**) to produce longer chains (**polymers**). By producing much bigger molecules, the physical state will often change from a gas to a solid. Ethylene (C_2H_4) (see Figure 3),

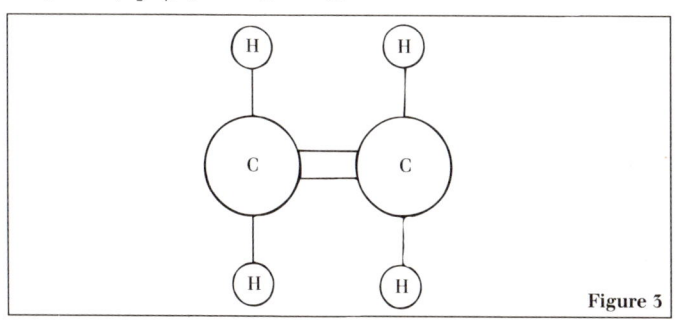

Figure 3

a gas, is an excellent monomer and is frequently used in the plastics industry as the basis for constructing long polymer chains. Energy is added to the system, in the form of heat and pressure, to force the monomers to begin to combine. This process, called polymerisation, is a chemical reaction because chemical bonds are broken and reformed. The reaction can be speeded up by the use of substances called **catalysts**. In effect, the new polymer is formed out of monomers like stringing beads to make a necklace. In the case of ethylene, the process leads to the formation of a resin called 'polythene'. Others formed by this process include 'polystyrene', 'polyvinyl' and 'polypropylene'. Different base monomers, or the introduction of a different monomer (known as condensation **polymerisation** because water is a by-product of the process), will lead to the formation of plastics with different physical properties such as nylon and polyester.

By changing the base monomer, the length of the polymer and any additional chemical elements bonded to the carbon chain 'backbone', the properties of the plastic can be changed. By making the polymer form in coils, the plastic can be made to be elastic (rubber bands are made from an elastomer plastic). Among the other chemical elements that are used to form short side chains are nitrogen, silicon and chlorine. Silicon can be used to improve the elasticity of a plastic (the silicon in bathroom sealant, for example); but chlorine, in the form of polyvinyl chloride (PVC), makes a plastic much more heat resistant and harder. Polymers tend to be formed in a dense tangled mass (rather like spaghetti), which means that they have a high tensile strength but are difficult to mould.

There are two basic forms of plastic which react to heat differently. Thermoplastics can be repeatedly melted and remoulded – the bonds between the polymers are relatively weak and easily broken and reformed on cooling. Thermosetting plastics, on the other hand, can only be moulded once. The bonds between the polymers are much stronger and form a 3-D lattice so that once moulded to shape, the object is effectively one giant molecule!

Why you need to know these facts

When a new material is made, chemical bonds are broken and reformed in different combinations – this process will either require heat or produce heat (or more precisely energy). The practical outcome of this as far as the children are concerned is that new materials are formed when mixtures are cooked or burnt (either using or releasing heat). This will help the children to appreciate the chemistry that continually happens around them.

Vocabulary

Catalyst – a substance that speeds up or increases a chemical reaction.

Coagulate – bunching together of protein molecules.

Combustion – reaction between a hydrocarbon and oxygen to produce carbon dioxide, water and heat.

Endothermic reaction – one that requires heat to occur.

Exothermic reaction – one that transfers heat to the local environment.

Monomer – a relatively small molecule made from a few atoms.

Polymer – a long chain of chemically bonded monomers.

Polymerisation – the process of combining monomers to form polymers.

- It takes 11kg of air to combust 1kg of coal.
- About 15 million chemical compounds have been identified and recorded – with a further 2000 being identified each day. Of these, only about 6500 are produced commercially.

Thunder makes milk go sour.
Leaving milk out in a warm environment, which encourages the microbes to multiply, makes it go sour. Thunderstorms, particularly in the summer, occur when warm and cooler air meet so it is just a coincidence that the weather conditions that produce a summer storm are also ideal for curdling milk – the same could be said of central heating (as a cause of curdling not summer storms)!

Why do you blow on a fire to 'get it going' but blow a candle out?
Blowing gently on or fanning a small fire will give it a greater supply of oxygen to work with and so will encourage the reaction. However, blowing hard will take the heat away and stop the reaction, putting the fire out.

Cooking (observing, recording)
Working in small, supervised groups, the children can observe the effect of heating different foodstuffs. In particular, observing eggs and cake mixtures as they are heated in a microwave can be very revealing.

Plaster of Paris (observing, recording)
Placing a small amount of plaster of Paris in a sandwich bag will allow each child to hold and mould their own. As the plaster quickly sets it will give off heat.

Candle watching (observation, recording)
Allowing a small group of children to observe a naked night light flame under strictly controlled and supervised conditions will allow the children to observe the different parts of the flame (see Figure 4). The blue base of the flame is where the wax vapour is completely combusted due to the plentiful supply of oxygen at this level. The central part of the flame directly over the wick will be darker due to the unburned wax vapour contained within it. The brighter part

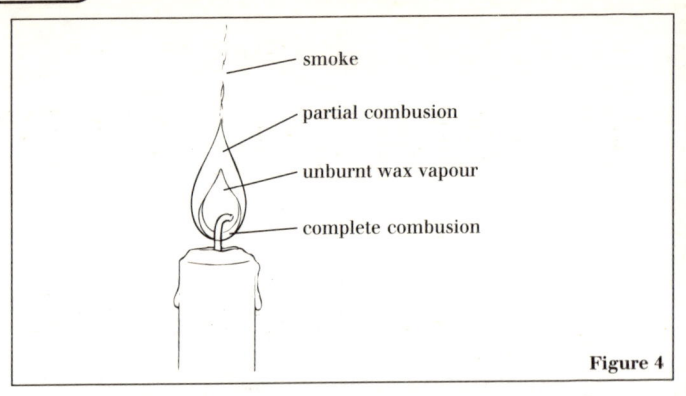

smoke

partial combusion

unburnt wax vapour

complete combusion

Figure 4

that surrounds this does not receive a good supply of oxygen so some of the vapour is only partially combusted, allowing some of it to form into molecules of soot.

Ceramics (observing, comparing)

Using a collection of different types of pottery, both fired and unfired, ask individuals to describe and compare the differences. Focus on the texture and feel of the materials – be wary of sharp edges. While ceramics are hard, unfired pottery will crumble and be dusty because the particles are not firmly bonded to each other.

Resources

Cooking equipment and ingredients
Dairy produce and milk
Collections of manufactured materials (particularly plastics)
Plaster of Paris
Plastic bags
Various secondary sources to research chemical reactions.

References

Children's Britannica (also online)
Multimedia CD-ROM encyclopaedia (such as *Encarta*)
Dorling Kindersley *Science Encyclopedia* CD-ROM

Chapter 6
CHANGING EARTH

The ideas contained in the primary curriculum concerning the nature of the Earth's crust are ones that are found in geography, but are included here to assist with the development of understanding the processes involved from a scientific perspective. The key ideas to be developed are that:

1. The Earth's crust is relatively thin, and its chemical composition is different from that of the interior of the planet.
2. Rocks change through a cycle of formation and erosion.
3. **Volcanoes** are active where the crust is thin.
4. **Earthquakes** are indications of movements of the crust.

Changing Earth concept chain
See 'The nature of "stuff" concept chain' on page 12 for general comments.

KS1
● Human habitation of the Earth is concerned with a very thin layer on the surface of the planet.
● The surface of the Earth is made up of many different types of rock.
● Volcanoes and earthquakes are the effects of movements on the Earth's surface.

KS2

● The Earth's crust represents only a relatively thin layer on its surface.
● Rocks can be categorised by how they were formed.
● The crust is thicker in some places than others.
● The crust moves around on a much thicker layer of **molten** rock.
● Where the crust is very thin the molten rock can seep through to form volcanoes.
● Earthquakes occur where parts of the crust move next to each other.

KS3

● Rocks laid down in strata are called **sedimentary** rocks.
● When sedimentary rocks are subjected to heat and extreme pressure they are changed into harder, **metamorphic** rocks.
● **Igneous** rocks form as molten rock cools.
● The Earth's crust is constantly moving but very slowly over extremely long timescales.

Concept 1: Scratching the surface

Subject facts

Humans are very much surface dwellers on planet Earth. All of the life that we are aware of is packed into a very limited region. From the deepest ocean (Pacific – 11km) to the highest mountain (Everest – 9km) there is only a difference of 20km. Even the **troposphere**, which contains almost all of our weather, extends between only 10km (at the Poles) and 16km (at the equator) above sea level. More than 50% of our air is within 5.5km of sea level. These numbers may seem quite large but not when you consider that the Earth is 12 760km in diameter. To appreciate the difference between 20km and 12 760km, let's scale things down to a more manageable size. If we take the Earth to be a circle of 30cm diameter, the ocean floor to the mountain-top will be less than 0.5mm. If you were actually to draw this circle you would need a pretty sharp pencil! The troposphere would be an extra 0.25mm – only a slightly blunter pencil! In terms of smoothness, this planet Earth is pretty smooth – the standard for snooker balls allows them to be proportionally rougher! If you were able to handle the Earth as a 30cm sphere you would just be able to make out the surface variations by touch – you would certainly be aware of damp patches or condensation on the surface (or 'oceans' as we call them).

This surface layer of the Earth is not rigidly fixed in place – and I am not just talking of the oceans here – the Earth does move, albeit rather slowly. The Earth's crust (see Figure 1) is just a surface skin, between 5 and 50km thick,

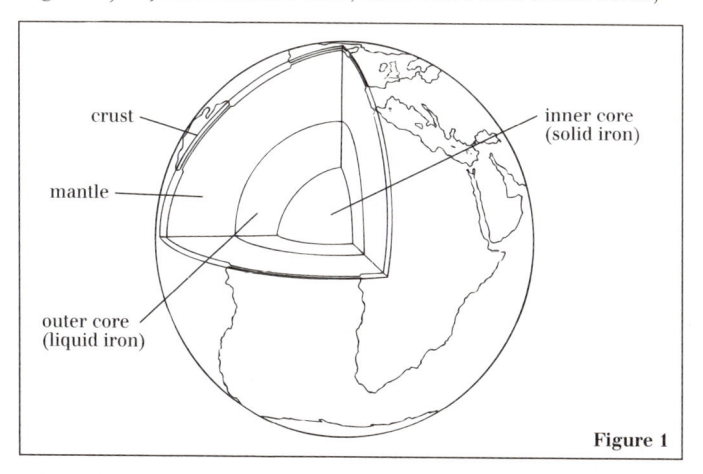

crust
mantle
outer core (liquid iron)
inner core (solid iron)

Figure 1

where the rocks have cooled sufficiently to solidify. The Earth is described as having five concentric, progressively denser, layers. The outermost is the gaseous atmosphere followed by the **hydrosphere** (all the surface water, for example oceans). The remaining three layers are the **lithosphere** (crust), **mantle** (2900km thick) and **core** (7500km in diameter). The mantle and core are very hot but due to the pressure they are under they have both solid and liquid properties. Currents deep within the Earth cause portions of the surface to move – even at a rate of as much as 2cm per year. This means that some parts of the continents have circled the globe twice since they were first formed.

Only 200 million years ago (the Earth has existed 23 times as long as this!) all the continents were together in one land mass called Pangaea, which split into Laurasia in the north and Gondwanaland in the south and then split and drifted again to leave the continents in their present positions. Over the next 50 million years Alaska will run into north-east Russia, the Mediterranean Sea will disappear as Africa and Europe merge and Australia will hurtle into the equatorial Pacific.

The crust of the Earth tends to be thickest in mountainous regions and thinnest where the ocean is deep. Around the Earth, at the points where these continental plates came into contact, internal heat from the planet can escape in the form of volcanoes, lava flows or hot springs. At its iron core, the Earth has a temperature of about 6650°C, which cools the nearer you get to the surface.

Why you need to know these facts

To instil in the children a sense of the scale of the habitable part of the Earth (the surface) it is important to develop an understanding of just how thin the crust actually is.

Vocabulary

Core – iron-based central portion of the Earth which is so hot and under so much pressure it acts like both a liquid and a solid.

Earthquake – a release of built up stresses caused by the movement of the Earth's crust.

Hydrosphere – the Earth's layer of surface water (mainly oceans and polar ice caps).

Igneous – rocks formed from cooling magma.

Lithosphere – surface crust of the Earth, 5 to 50km thick.

Mantle – the semi-liquid rock layer between the core and the crust.

Metamorphic – rocks that have been transformed by heat and pressure.

Molten – a solid that has been turned (melted) into a liquid through heating.

Sedimentary – a rock formed by particles being deposited in layers.

Troposphere – that part of the atmosphere that contains most of our weather.

Volcano – a conical mound formed by the expulsion of volcanic material.

Amazing facts

● The Atlantic is getting 2.5cm wider each year.
● The Earth's crust only accounts for 0.5% of the Earth's mass.
● Many of the Earth's volcanoes can be found on the Pacific Rim. The Hawaiian islands were, in fact, created by volcanic activity.
● The largest known volcano is not on Earth, but Mars. It is called Olympus Mons.
● The strongest earthquake ever recorded happened in 1960 in Gansu, China. It measured 8.5 on the Richter scale.

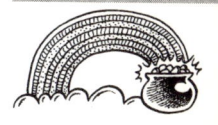

There are monsters living in the centre of the Earth.
Journey to the Centre of the Earth by Jules Verne (1864) was
written at a time when very little was known about the
inner workings of the Earth. Now we know for certain that
no such places within the Earth can exist – but this does not
prevent some form of exotic life from developing deep down
inside the Earth. However, it will certainly be nothing like
anything we have ever seen before!

Questions

Is there a giant magnet in the centre of the Earth?
Not a magnet as such. The solid iron core is thought to
move within the liquid iron outer core. The friction between
the two sets up an electromagnetic field similar in some
ways to a dynamo. This is what produces the Earth's
magnetic field.

Teaching ideas

A matter of scale (comparison)

Through discussion, find out the ideas that the children
hold concerning the structure of the Earth. Encourage them
to work as groups to explain and present their ideas to the
rest of the class as drawings. Use the parameters described
above to produce a scale drawing or model (using different
coloured play dough, for example) of the Earth with which
the children can compare their ideas.

Concept 2: Rocks

Subject facts

There are basically two different ways in which rocks are
formed – by cooling of molten rock (or lava) or by
compacting of deposits (sedimentation) (see Figure 2).

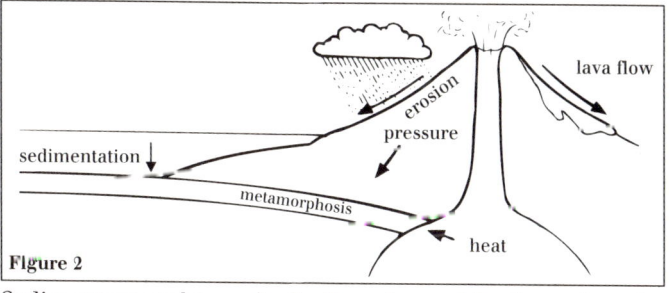

Figure 2

Sedimentary rocks can be further changed by the action of
heat and immense pressures that can be found deep in the
crust to form metamorphic rocks. There is a constant 'rock

cycle' caused by the erosion and formation of surface rocks – the timescale here is measured in tens of thousands of years. The process of erosion is addressed in Chapter 7, 'Changing weather'.

Sedimentary rocks

These rocks take a long time to form. They are made from the eroded particles of older rocks of all types of organic matter. The classification of these rocks is usually on the basis of the texture or grain size. Conglomerates are made from pebbles or even boulders of other rocks cemented together by sediment. They vary tremendously depending upon the size, proportion and nature of the pebbles. Medium-grained sedimentary rocks include sandstone, which has a gritty feel to it. Fine-grained varieties, such as shale, are often made from clay particles that have a diameter of less than 1mm.

Another form of classification is by chemical composition. Limestone and chalk, which contain over 50% calcium carbonate, mainly from the shells of dead sea creatures, is a carbonate. As a rock it can be rather soft and crumbly. A particularly useful form of sedimentary rock is the combustible carbonaceous group, which consists mainly of compacted vegetation – it's also known as 'coal'.

Sedimentary rocks have quite a range of uses: sandstone and limestone are used for building, and shale and limestone in cement and fertiliser, for example.

Metamorphic rocks

These occur when rocks that have been formed by other means, mainly by sedimentation, are subjected to heat and pressure as a result of burial in the Earth's crust. The main outcome of this is a harder, denser rock. There are three grades of metamorphism: low, medium and high. The high grade ones are subject to the greatest change from the parent rock, almost completely reforming and crystallising. The low grade metamorphic rocks are the most common since they are most often found on or near the surface. The three key sedimentary rocks (limestone, shale and sandstone) are metamorphosed into marble, slate and quartzite – all much harder and more durable than the originals.

Igneous rocks

These are the only rocks that begin as a molten liquid – the volcanic material called **magma** when it is under the crust and **lava** when it reaches the surface. They tend to be classified on the basis of where they formed. If they solidified underground they are known as intrusive and because they cooled slowly the crystals that form will be much larger than the **extrusive** igneous rock that forms as it rapidly cools on the surface.

Granite is a good example of an **intrusive** igneous rock – outcrops can often be found where the surrounding, softer rocks have been eroded away. The extrusive form is more common on the Earth's surface. It can vary tremendously from pumice, which is formed from very viscous, gas-filled lava to produce a rock that floats in water, to obsidian, which has a black, glassy consistency. The most common igneous rock is basalt, which reaches the surface through volcanic vents and flows over the land surface.

Hardness

As well as varying in density, chemical composition and mode of formation, rocks also vary in hardness. Moh's hardness scale, named after the German geologist Friedrich Moh, is used as a comparative test of the hardness of rocks. The scale, 1 to 10, relates only to particular rocks and minerals and their rank order within the scale – 4 is not twice as hard as 2, for example.

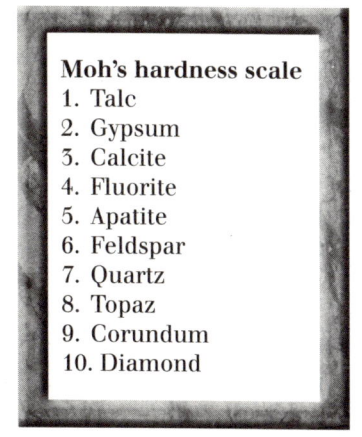

Moh's hardness scale
1. Talc
2. Gypsum
3. Calcite
4. Fluorite
5. Apatite
6. Feldspar
7. Quartz
8. Topaz
9. Corundum
10. Diamond

1 and 2 can be marked by a fingernail, 3 by a copper coin, 4 and 5 by a knife blade, 6 to 0 will scratch glass and 10 – virtually anything!

Soil

Soil basically consists of different but small particles of rock mixed with a range of organic substances such as decomposing leaf litter and micro-organisms. Soil types are considered in Chapter 4, 'Mixing and separating'.

The sorting of rocks according to their observable and testable characteristics can be taken a step further by an understanding of how they were formed. The children can be encouraged to begin to appreciate the timescales involved in the processes as well.

Vocabulary

Extrusive – igneous rock formed on the surface of the Earth.
Intrusive – igneous rock formed by slow cooling within the Earth.
Lava – magma that has reached the surface.
Magma – molten rock beneath the Earth's surface.

Amazing facts

● While over 75% of the Earth's exposed surface is made of sedimentary rock, it makes up only 5% of the crust layer.
● Oxygen (46%) and silicone (27%) are the most common elements in the crust.
● The Deccan trap, a basalt rock in western India formed by a lava flow, covers an area over 200 000km^2.

Common misconceptions

Rocks are older than life on Earth.
Although some may be, there are many examples that show that some rocks have formed quite recently. Where rocks form as a result of volcanic action they must be very new – currently a new island is growing in the south Pacific, constructed of cooling lava. The discovery of fossils – the imprint in sedimentary rocks of long dead animals and plants – was one of the discoveries that encouraged the development of a set of geological theories to explain sedimentation.

Rocks never change.
Okay, I agree that you may get bored waiting for a rock to 'do something', but in fact the changes are happening, although they occur very slowly. On a very long timescale there is a 'rock cycle' (see Figure 2) whereby rocks are formed, eroded and worn down by the action of the atmosphere and used to form the basis of new rocks. Different types of rocks are eroded at different rates in different environmental conditions. The key eroding elements are the actions of water (or ice), wind and changing temperature.

When did the last rocks form?

Rocks are in a continuous cycle of formation and erosion, although mostly this happens so slowly that we don't even notice. Some, like those that have been extruded from a volcanic vent, are forming all of the time. As you are reading this, lava is solidifying in some part of the world – in fact a lot of it forms on the ocean floors. Sedimentary rock, though, takes much longer to form. Bones of animals that died hundreds or tens of millions of years ago can be found as fossils in sedimentary rocks. Other fossils are only 10 000 years old.

Rock samples (observing, comparing)

Ask children to compare and sort rocks according to their observable features. Some groups of children might be able to prepare a sorting key, where individual rock samples can be identified by reference to a list of prepared and standard questions. Dripping water or vinegar on to rocks to see if they are either porous or react to a mild acid is another useful test (limestone does).

Hard rocks (observing, testing)

Each group of children can place a selection of five or so rock samples in order of hardness by testing each rock against the others. For each test the children should note which rock marks and which rock is marked. The groups can then compare the order of their samples. If they haven't all got the same rocks, can they place them in one rank order for the class?

Concept 3: Moving crust

Although the human race has always been aware of volcanoes and earthquakes, it wasn't until early last century (1912) that a unifying theory was put forward for why these phenomena occur. The German scientist Alfred Wegener proposed the theory of continental drift by comparing the similarities in the coastlines of west Africa and eastern South America and deducing that the crust of the Earth is made from a series of **tectonic plates** which are constantly moving in relation to each other. The geology of the continents was similar, but how did they get so far apart? Where was the 'extra' ocean floor coming from? The

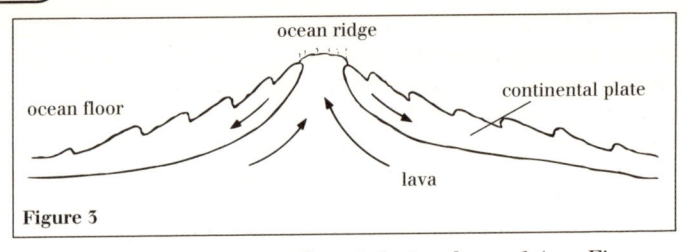

ocean ridge

ocean floor

continental plate

lava

Figure 3

answer is that new ocean floor is being formed (see Figure 3). In some parts of the world the crust is thinner than others, particularly on ocean floors. Here the magma beneath the crust is able to force its way up, forming mounds in the ocean floor. The magma breaks through to form a new piece of sea bed, so forcing the plates, and the continents that ride on them, further apart. Clearly not all of the continents can be moving apart, some must be moving closer. While the Atlantic is getting wider, the Pacific is narrowing. Here the Pacific plate is being pushed under the American plate. As the Pacific plate (see Figure 4)

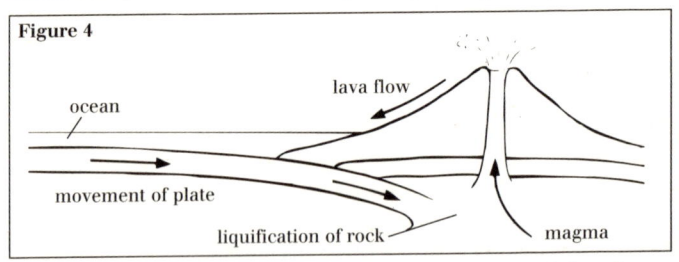

Figure 4

lava flow

ocean

movement of plate

liquification of rock

magma

slides under the American, in a process called **subduction**, the rock re-liquefies as it is heated under pressure. This magma will often force its way to the surface through vents and volcanoes – like those in the Andes on the western edge of South America. The Andes are an example of 'fold mountains', caused by the rumpling of the Earth's crust as the South American plate collides with the Pacific plate. This range continues into the Rockies in North America. A particularly fine example is the Himalayan range, formed as the Indian sub-continent rammed into Asia in a series of prolonged collisions between 30 and 50 million years ago.

Volcanoes

Volcanoes can usually be found where one tectonic plate is sliding under another, such as south-east Asia and Japan. Iceland, though, is expanding because it finds itself on the top of an oceanic ridge where tectonic plates are moving away from each other – a particularly active volcanic region.

Not all volcanoes are the same. It very much depends upon the viscosity or thickness of the lava, the pressure that it is under and the nature of the surface material. Lava can vary from the consistency of cold toothpaste (rhyolitic lava) to warm syrup (basaltic lava) – at a temperature of anything up to 1200°C. A very fluid lava which is able to find its way to the surface through natural fissures in the crust is likely to provide a steady flow. Rather than a conical volcano, a basaltic type of molten emission may form a nearly flat plateau. If there is no 'easy' route to the surface and the magma is more viscous, the magma pocket will begin to expand (see Figure 5)

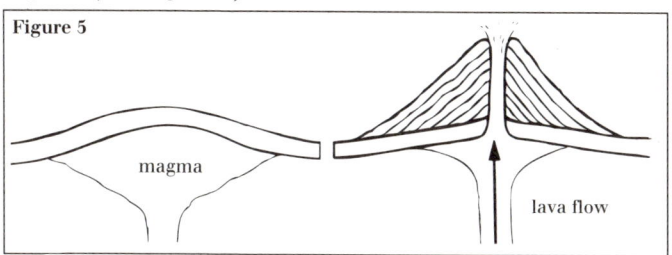

Figure 5

magma

lava flow

and push the surface up to form a dome. The pressure will continue to grow until the rhyolitic lava finally bursts through to the surface. The violent release of pressure may throw volcanic gases, rock fragments and **pyroclasts** (lumps of lava) a great distance.

Different types of lava also form different forms of rock. Thin, basaltic lava will form dense, uniform rock, while thicker rhyolitic lava may have more dissolved gas in it, allowing it to form spongy silicate rock such as pumice. Overall, rhyolitic lava forms much less uniform rock.

If the matter expelled from the volcano is mainly ash, the cone that begins to build up can be very steep sided, but relatively small – certainly no more than a few hundred metres tall. Lava flows, like those on the Hawaiian Islands, tend not to be explosive but cause extended and extensive build-up of volcanic material. These volcanoes are conical but they have a very wide base relative to their height. Mauna Loa, the volcano on Hawaii, has a cone 120km by 50km and reaches a height of 4170m.

Earthquakes

As the tectonic plates in its surface move, the Earth shudders. It is not a smooth, free-flowing movement but a series of judders. Generally the longer it is between these judders, the bigger the next movement is. Most earthquakes occur along geological fault lines, such as the San Andreas

Fault in California. Here two plates are rubbing against each other causing horizontal movement. Nearby there is also a subduction fault where one plate is slipping under another, causing a vertical displacement. In an earthquake in Japan in 1923 the seabed in part of Sagami Bay dropped by 400m.

Earthquakes are measured on the Richter Scale, after Charles Richter, who devised the scale in 1935 to describe the strength of Californian eathquakes. This scale is based upon how much the Earth moves 100km from the epicentre of an earthquake. As these movements can vary as much as from 0.000 01mm to 1m (as measured by a **seismograph**) the scale used is not a linear one. A 4 on the scale is ten times as great as a 3 (the Earth moves ten times as much). Zero on the scale is not 'no movement', just ten times less than a 1.

The energy released during an earthquake is 32 times greater for each unit up the scale. So while earthquakes of 4 are quite common in some places on the globe, there may be only one of 8 or above per year. It is thought that the crust cannot store sufficient energy to release a 10 earthquake, though it is calculated that a 12 would split the Earth in two! The energy released by the atomic bomb dropped on Hiroshima was equivalent to a 4.3 eathquake – it would take 66 million of these bombs, all exploded at the same place at the same time, to reproduce the largest earthquake ever recorded (8.5 – Chile, 1960).

Why you need to know these facts

Earthquakes and volcanoes frequently have an adverse effect on the local human inhabitants and so are described in the daily news. In many places, buildings need to be specially designed and constructed to ensure that they can withstand the forces of all but the strongest earthquakes. An understanding of why these events occur is important in beginning to understand the science behind the news.

Vocabulary

Pyroclast – a lump of hot volcanic material.
Seismograph – a meter that measures movements in the Earth.
Subduction – when one tectonic plate is pushed beneath another.
Tectonic plate – a portion of the surface of the Earth which moves relative to other parts of the Earth's surface.

Amazing facts

- When Mount Saint Helens erupted in 1980 it threw a cloud of hot ashes and gas 19km into the atmosphere.
- The eruption of Tambora (Indonesia) in 1815 ejected over 150km³ of material. Most of the world's volcanoes are in this part of south-east Asia.
- A lava flow over 15 million years ago in North America was over 48km long. The longest in recent times was one of 70km in Iceland in 1783.
- There are about 500 000 detectable Earth movements a year. Of these, 1000 cause actual damage.

Common misconceptions

Earthquakes don't happen in the UK.
Yes they do, but fortunately not very big ones. Earthquakes with epicentres in the UK do take place, though strong earthquakes in other parts of the world can also be detected here. The 'famously' destructive East Anglian earthquake of 1884 damaged 1250 buildings (at a cost of £12 000!). The Warwick earthquake of September 2000 was the strongest in Britain for over ten years (4.2 on the Richter scale).

Questions

Why do some earthquakes cause more damage?
To begin with, some earthquakes are stronger than others. But if an earthquake occurs in a lightly populated area the damage is likely to be less. If it centres on a heavily populated area the destruction will be largely dependent upon the level of preparation and technology that has gone into the construction of the buildings. In rich countries where there are earthquakes the buildings are strengthened to withstand tremors, but in poorer countries, or where the buildings are older, they are often unable to withstand the forces involved so more people become casualties.

Teaching ideas

Volcano (demonstration)
Build your 'volcano' as in Figure 6.

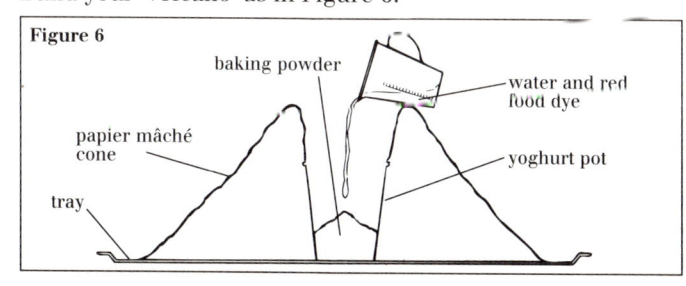

Figure 6

baking powder

water and red food dye

papier mâché cone

yoghurt pot

tray

A mixture of bicarbonate of soda and citric acid crystals or baking powder alone will produce a delightful amount of foam when water is poured onto it. Adding red food dye to the water will add greater 'authenticity' to the 'lava' as it bubbles over the edge of the cone.

Earthquakes (research)

Ask groups of children to brainstorm questions about earthquakes and then research the answers using encyclopaedia and multimedia packages (such as *Encarta*). Present their findings to the class as a display or a multimedia presentation.

Resources

Multimedia CD-ROM encyclopaedia (such as *Encarta*)
Rock samples
Rock testing kits

Chapter 7
CHANGING WEATHER

The ideas contained in the primary curriculum concerning weather begin to appear only during Key Stage 2 geography but a scientific understanding is necessary to appreciate the causal relationships. Seasonal change of weather and climatic change due to latitude is fundamentally linked to the physics of the movement of the Earth around the Sun, concepts which are examined in Chapter 7 of *Physical Processes*. The key ideas to be developed here are that:

1. The water cycle is a key component of the weather.
2. Weather fronts and systems lead to changes in the weather.
3. Seasons and climate changes are due to a combination of geographic position and inclination of the Sun.
4. The landscape may change on a longer cycle due to the direct and indirect effects of the weather.

Changing weather concept chain

See 'The nature of "stuff" concept chain' on page 12 for general comments.

KS1

● The Sun warms the Earth.
● Rain (snow and hail) falls from clouds.
● Wind is moving air.

● Temperature and weather vary on a seasonal basis.
● It is possible to record and predict the weather by making direct observations and measurements.

KS2
● Water evaporates into the atmosphere and can form clouds.
● As it cools, the water in the atmosphere condenses to form clouds and **precipitation**.
● As the Sun warms the air the air rises, drawing in surrounding cooler air (wind).
● Climate depends upon the amount of warmth received from the Sun, altitude and proximity to oceans.
● The changing inclination and heat from the Sun causes seasonal change.
● Heat, wind and water affect the nature of the landscape and cause erosion.
● Weather measuring devices and satellite observations can be used to forecast short-term weather patterns.

KS3
● All weather is caused by the heat of the Sun.
● The rate of atmospheric evaporation is dependent upon the air temperature and availability of water.
● Differences in air pressure determine the strength of wind.
● The rotation of the Earth causes weather systems to move.
● Differing air temperatures give rise to weather fronts.
● Different climates experience a different range of seasonal changes.
● The erosion of the landscape by the action of weather takes place over a long time period.

Concept 1: Water cycle

Subject facts

Storage
The vast majority of the water on our planet is stored in the oceans (see 'Amazing facts'). Each day 1200km^3 of water evaporates (see Chapter 3, 'Changing state', page 67) into the atmosphere and the same amount falls back to earth. If evaporation ceased now it would take ten days for the water currently in the atmosphere to precipitate out. The main source that water evaporates from is the ocean but other significant sources (in terms of their impact on the planet

and humans in particular) are plant transpiration (see Chapter 5, 'Green plants', in *Pocket Guides: Life Processes and Living Things*) and fresh water sources on land.

Evaporation

It is the heat provided by the Sun that causes water on the surface of the Earth to evaporate. The rate at which water is able to evaporate is dependent upon temperature, intensity of sunlight, wind speed, moisture content of the ground and the intensity of sunlight. On average a depth of about 1m of water evaporates per year across the face of the Earth – though this does vary from almost zero at the Poles to over 4m around the Gulf Stream in the Gulf of Mexico. The rate at which water evaporates decreases as humidity increases to a point where no more water can evaporate at that air temperature. When the air temperature falls slightly, as it does in the afternoon in the tropics, or as the air is pushed to higher, cooler regions of the atmosphere to go over mountains, the water vapour will condense and fall back to earth.

Precipitation

The process of precipitation starts as water vapour in the air (invisible) condenses to form larger droplets or ice crystals that group together to form clouds. There are several main types of cloud (see Figure 1) which are classified according to their altitude and shape. Approximately 25% of precipitation falls on land. The land areas that receive the most rainfall, on average, tend to be those in densely forested, tropical areas where plant transpiration

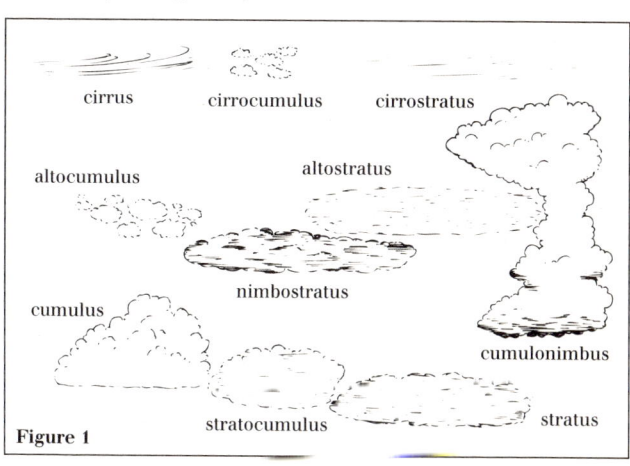

cirrus · cirrocumulus · cirrostratus · altocumulus · altostratus · nimbostratus · cumulus · cumulonimbus · stratocumulus · stratus

Figure 1

greatly increases the moisture content of the air, and temperature changes set off daily deluges of rain.

Run-off

Of the 300km^3 of **precipitation** falling daily on the land, two-thirds will evaporate (either directly or through plant transpiration or animal usage) leaving 100km³ to flow back into the ocean via river systems. The Amazon basin alone accounts for 15% of this run-off. As the water flows over the land it shapes it through the erosion (see below, page 134) of rocks and the transportation of soil and organic material.

Why you need to know these facts

The action of the Sun in causing water to evaporate (see Chapter 3, 'Changing state') into the atmosphere and warm air to rise and later to cool causing the moisture to condense and fall back to earth is fundamental to an understanding of the processes of weather.

Vocabulary

Precipitation – water vapour in the atmosphere returning to liquid form (rain, snow, hail, mist).

Amazing facts

● There are approximately 1.4 billion km³ of water on Earth, of which 97% is salty sea water.
● Of the 36 million km³ of fresh water, 28 million km³ is held in the ice caps, 7.8 million km³ in the ground and only 120 000km³ in rivers and lakes (3% of the fresh water).
● At any one time there will be 12 000km³ of fresh water in the atmosphere (water vapour).

Common misconceptions

Water is evaporated from the sea, it forms clouds, the rain falls on mountains and the water runs back along rivers to the sea.
This is not exactly false, but all too often this over-simplification of the cycle can become embedded. Water also evaporates from lakes, puddles and tropical forests and although mountainous regions do tend to be quite wet, they are not the only place where rain falls. Water is also absorbed by living things or by permeable rocks – rivers don't have it all! Some idea of the scale of the proportions involved in the various stages of the cycle (as described above) should give a better appreciation of what actually happens in practice. Children should be asked to consider all of the alternative routes that rainfall might take (from evaporating puddles, to human use and beyond).

Clouds are like the steam from a kettle.
Boiling and evaporation (see page 67) are both ways in which liquid water can be changed into a gas – but the gas (water vapour) is transparent. The white stuff is a collection of small water droplets that form as water vapour cools. They are so tiny they are kept up in the air. Unlike the cloud of condensed water vapour from a kettle, the clouds in the sky are much colder.

Why is the ground often wet in the morning even though it hasn't rained?

Dew forms when the cold night air forces the water vapour held in the air to condense. A similar thing happens when you breathe out on a cold day – you can see a cloud appear as the water vapour in your breath condenses. As the ground cools down quickly at night the water vapour condenses into water droplets, and this is what can be seen on grass, for instance. Frost is a similar thing, only it occurs when it is cold enough for the droplets to turn into ice crystals.

Cloud observations (observation, recording, inferring, predicting)

Encourage the children to keep an individual, group or class record of the types of cloud they can see in different weather conditions (still, windy, showery, drizzle, snow). Ask them to make predictions about the chances of different types of precipitation from the clouds that they can see.

Concept 2: Weather fronts

Moisture content

Warm air can hold more water as water vapour than cold air. As warm air is cooled the vapour condenses to form clouds and if cooled further it will lead to rain. So warm air tends to be more humid and cooler air drier. As warm and cool air masses meet, clouds are formed out of the water vapour held in the warmer air.

Cold front

As a moving mass of cold air moves up against a mass of warm air (Figure 2a), the cold air, being denser, will tend to slide underneath the warm, moist air. The warm air is

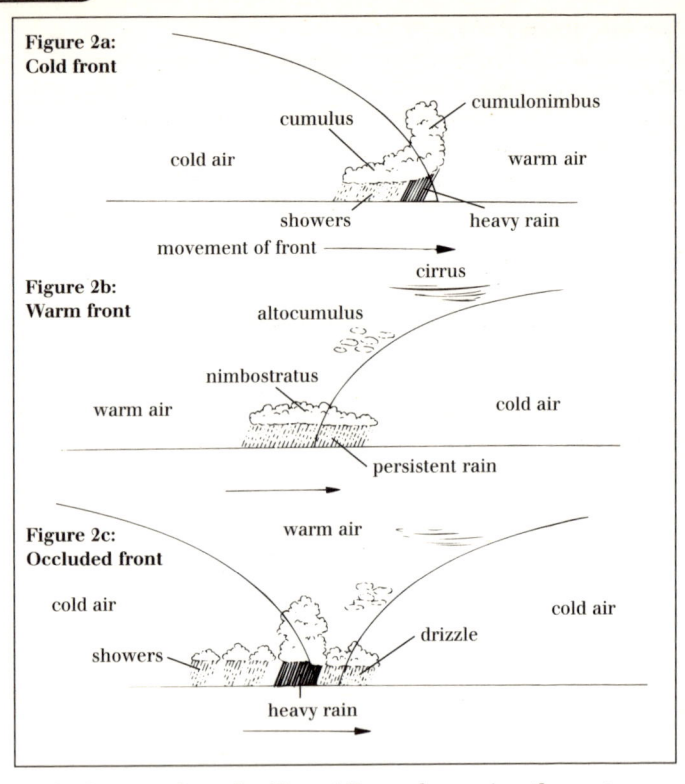

pushed upwards and will rapidly cool, causing the water vapour to condense. This rapid cooling will lead to the formation of storm clouds (**cumulonimbus**), and the wind strength will increase and the temperature drop. As the front actually arrives, the rain will fall as a downfall – if the cold air is cold enough it may include hail or even fall as snow. After the front has passed, the air will be cooler and less windy, though there may be a few short sharp showers as the cumulus remnants of the large storm clouds go over.

Warm front

Alternatively, a mass of warm air may run into a mass of cold air (Figure 2b). As it does so it will tend to rise over it. Clouds will form high in the sky – first **cirrus** than possibly **altocumulus**. This is a warning of rain to follow. The wind strength may increase as the sky darkens as the cloud thickens and becomes progressively lower. A blanket of **nimbostratus** cloud will arrive just ahead of the front, along with steady, continuous rain. The rain may persist as drizzle for several hours before the front passes and the warmer air finally arrives.

Occluded front

Generally **cold fronts** move faster than warm ones so it is often possible for a cold front to 'catch up' with a **warm front** to form an **occluded** front (Figure 2c). Here the warmer air is forced up and above the colder air. This often results in a band of drizzle followed by heavier rain and then showers before the sky finally clears.

Weather systems

Differences in atmospheric air pressure are denoted on weather maps by **isobars**. These are lines drawn to connect up points of equal pressure – the same way that contour lines (isoclines) join up points of the same height on a relief map. These isobars never cross. The closer they are together the steeper the pressure differential – and this usually means the stronger the wind (see Figure 3).

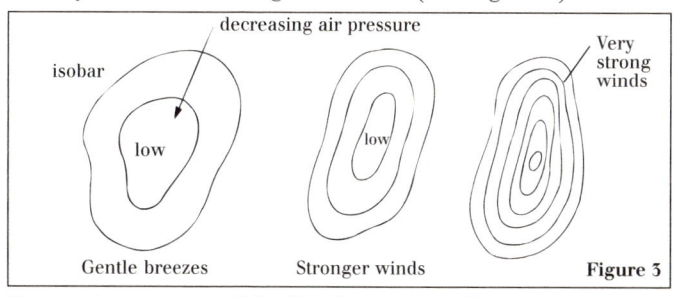

decreasing air pressure

isobar

Very strong winds

low

low

Gentle breezes   Stronger winds   **Figure 3**

Due to the rotation of the Earth and the effect that this has on the movement of the air, winds tend to spiral into low-pressure areas. These are masses of warmer air which are less dense than the surrounding cooler air – the warm air rises and the cooler air flows in. In the northern hemisphere the air flows in an anti-clockwise direction, spiralling in towards the centre of the low pressure area. In the southern hemisphere it flows in a clockwise direction. This is due to the rotation of the Earth and the effect that this has on the surface of the planet. From directly above the north pole the Earth would appear to rotate anti-clockwise and from above the South Pole, clockwise. It should be noted, though, that for the Coriolis effect (the direction taken by water running down a plughole), the northern and southern hemispheres are clockwise and anti-clockwise respectively. Sometimes, in tropical areas, when the air has been warmed considerably more than the surrounding air, the pressure difference is so great that the spiralling-in air can be made to move very quickly indeed. These **cyclonic** storm centres are known as **hurricanes** in the Caribbean and as **typhoons** in the Pacific.

Coastal weather

Coastal areas can have distinctly different weather systems due to the proximity of land and water. While water (the sea or ocean) maintains a reasonably consistent temperature throughout the year, the temperature of the land can change considerably during the day. In the morning the land will be cool, relative to the sea, and so the air over the land will be of a slightly higher pressure leading to off-shore breezes (from sea to land). After midday, when the land has been heated by the Sun, the air pressure differential will have been reversed, leading to on-shore breezes. When the land has cooled considerably overnight, morning off-shore breezes can lead to the formation of coastal mist or fog. These breezes can also disrupt the formation of frost by keeping the local temperature up.

Why you need to know these facts

The satellite weather map is now a familiar feature of all televised weather forecasts. It is now possible, with the guidance of the weather presenter, to gain some insights into the relationships between cloud masses and their movements, the wind speed and direction, and the position and type of **weather fronts**. The actual effects of air pressure differentials (isobars) can now be seen in sequential weather satellite pictures. An understanding of weather fronts is important for developing a scientific awareness of weather.

Vocabulary

Alto – middle clouds.

Cirrus – high clouds.

Cold front – cold air undercutting a mass of warm air (rain storm).

Cumulus – fluffy clouds.

Cyclone – a low air pressure area otherwise known as a depression.

Hurricane or **typhoon** – a severe cyclone.

Isobar – line joining up points of equal atmospheric pressure.

Nimbo/nimbus – rain bearing clouds (darker).

Occluded front – warm air trapped between two masses of cold air (drizzle then heavy rain).

Stratus – layer cloud.

Warm front – warm air rising over a mass of cold air (persistent rain).

Weather front – the border between air masses of different temperatures.

● Wind speeds of up to 350kmh⁻¹ have been recorded in hurricanes.
● A tropical storm on the island of Reunion in the Indian Ocean released 1.87m of rainfall in 24hrs in 1952.

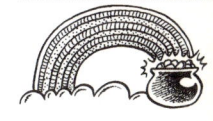

A cold front brings cold weather and a warm front warm weather.
Frontal weather systems bring rain! Warm air is capable of containing a higher proportion of water vapour than cold, so when a mass of cooler air comes into contact with moisture laden warmer air, the warmer air is cooled so it is unable to contain as much water vapour – so it rains. You may notice that, on a summer's evening, the temperature will drop just before a summer rainstorm, but this is linked more to the air releasing the water vapour that it holds than to the arrival of cold weather.

When it gets cloudy does it mean that it's going to rain?
Not always – it depends on the sort of cloud. White clouds tend not to cause rain as the water droplets are too far apart to form big enough drops to fall. Grey clouds (the darker the worse the rain) are the ones to watch out for – often they are low clouds (see Figure 1). Different types of cloud give different types of rain – dark, fluffy (cumulus) ones give short, sharp rainstorms, while dark banks of cloud (stratus) can give persistent rain or drizzle.

Weather watch (observation, prediction)
Have a class of children watch the section of a weather forecast showing satellite pictures of cloud movements (with the sound off). Discuss what this video tells you about the forthcoming weather – what are the important factors? (cloud movement – direction and speed, amount of cloud). Can you spot where the fronts are? Turn the sound up to check your interpretation.

Front watch (observation, prediction)
This is a similar idea to that above, only using a static weather map showing the frontal systems. Discuss the types of weather that are likely to be ahead of and behind these fronts.

Concept 3: Seasons and climate

Climate is a dependent of two key factors: heat and precipitation. There are five temperature determined climatic zones:

1. Tropical, with annual and monthly averages above 20°C
2. Subtropical, with 4 to 11 months above 20°C, and the balance between 10° and 20°C
3. Temperate, with 4 to 12 months at 10° to 20°C, and the rest cooler
4. Cold, with 1 to 4 months at 10° to 20°C, and the rest cooler
5. Polar, with 12 months below 10°C.

These can then be further divided by reference to the rainfall pattern:

1. Equatorial: rain throughout the year
2. Tropical: summer rain with winters dry
3. Semi-arid tropical: slight summer rain
4. Arid: dry throughout the year
5. Dry Mediterranean: slight winter rain
6. Mediterranean: winter rain, summers dry
7. Temperate: precipitation in all **seasons**
8. Polar: mainly dry in all seasons (though the existing snow will frequently be blown around).

The UK falls into the temperate band in both lists. Whilst both northern and central Australia fall into the subtropical band by temperature, the north has significant summer rains (tropical) while the central region is arid. Much of the difference is due to the location relative to water and prevailing wind and sea currents.

Position is all important

The weather you are likely to receive is dependent upon where you are on the Earth. The most significant factor is the amount of heat from the Sun that you receive and the next is how near you are to water. Water retains heat better than land and so moderates the temperature of the land that it is near. If there is no large body of water nearby, such as the middle of a large continent, the temperature can vary quite dramatically depending on the availability of heat from the Sun.

Generally speaking, due to the angle that the light and heat from the Sun strikes the Earth, the equatorial regions are hot and the polar ones are cold. So winds and their weather systems that come from the polar regions will be cold and those emanating from equatorial regions will be hotter. Also, weather systems travelling across oceans will tend to be mild (moderated by the temperature of the ocean) and wet, and those from continental areas will be dry and hot if the continent is hot, and cold if it is cold (see Figure 4a).

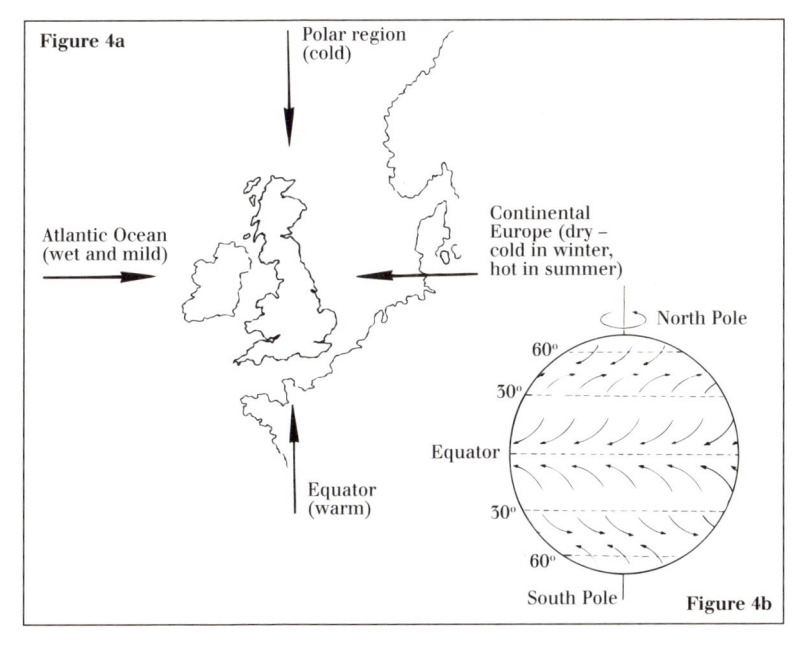

Figure 4a

Polar region (cold)

Atlantic Ocean (wet and mild)

Continental Europe (dry – cold in winter, hot in summer)

North Pole

Equator (warm)

60°
30°
Equator
30°
60°

South Pole

Figure 4b

Latitude

It would seem sensible to assume that the further away from the equator (and the closer to the polar regions) that you get, the colder the climate would get (see Chapter 7 'Earth in space' in *Physical Processes*), but it is not quite as simple as that. Ocean currents and prevailing winds also have a considerable effect (see Figure 4b). As the Earth spins anti-clockwise (from over the North Pole) – west to east – the winds blowing towards the warmer tropical regions tend to flow against the spin by flowing from the east to the west. Above 30° north and south of the equator, to counter this flow, the prevailing winds are from west to east. These prevailing westerly winds bring the moderating effect of the Atlantic Ocean to western Europe so the temperatures are higher in winter and lower in summer than they might otherwise be. New England, in the north-east of the USA, is approximately at the same latitude, but because its prevailing winds come from continental America it has much colder winters and warmer summers.

Altitude

The height above sea level has an effect on the likely weather – the higher up that you are the more likely it is to be colder than other places nearby at the same latitude.

Seasons

The terms 'summer' and 'winter' have meaning for us in western Europe because the amount of heat reaching us from the Sun does vary on a seasonal basis as the inclination of the Sun changes (see Chapter 7, 'Earth in space' in *Physical Processes*). But those living nearer the equator have a much reduced, if not non-existent, appreciation of these seasonal differences.

On the equator there is very little seasonal change as the Sun will only vary from slightly north to slightly south of overhead throughout the year. At the other extreme, in the polar regions, the Sun will change from visible in the sky to not visible in the sky on a six-monthly cycle. Even when the Sun is 'there' its inclination will be so low as to offer only a small amount of warmth to the ground.

Monsoon

The seasonal monsoon winds of the Indian Ocean are caused by seasonal pressure differences. The central Asian landmass warms and cools on a seasonal cycle – in the summer it is warm, in the winter cold. This means that in the summer a low-pressure area lies over much of central Asia. This draws air in (wind) from the surrounding oceans, including the Indian Ocean.

So in the northern hemisphere's summer, moisture-laden winds are drawn in across the Indian subcontinent (from a generally south-westerly direction) bringing rain (or a 'rainy season'). In the northern hemisphere winter, the air over central Asia cools, causing a high pressure area. Winds flow out from here bringing dry weather (there are no large bodies of water from which to gain moisture) to the Indian subcontinent (generally from the north-east).

Why you need to know these facts

Although they are different things, seasons and climate are combined here because children need to realise that different places in the world experience different climates and that each climate experiences different seasons. Hopefully understanding these variations will also help the children to understand the environmental basis of different cultures and lifestyles throughout different parts of the globe.

Climate – the long-term effect of the sun's light and heat on a particular part of the world.
Season – a period during the year having a particular climate.

● An island off the coast of Brazil in the southern Atlantic Ocean had a temperature range of only 13°C between 1911 and 1966 (surrounded by warm ocean).
● The town of Verkhoyanski, in eastern Russia, has recorded temperatures from –70°C to 36.7°C – a range of over 106°C (surrounded by land).

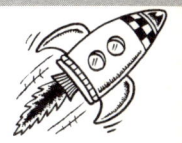

The further south you go the hotter it gets.
Yes, as long as you are heading in the direction of the equator – once past that, the further south you go the colder it will get. Children can build up the misconception that the South Pole is hot! Remind them that Antarctica is where most penguins come from.

Do all parts of the world have four seasons?
Only those parts of the world with latitudes of between 30° and 60° north and south of the equator have a true four-season year – which means mainly Europe and North America, as well as parts of Asia, with only the southern tips of Africa, South America and Australia/New Zealand having the southern hemisphere equivalent. Equatorial regions remain fairly constant throughout the year. The Arctic and Antarctic regions are also fairly constant throughout the year – cold – but have extremes of day and night, each lasting about six months at a time.

What's the weather like? (research, comparisons)
In groups, ask the children to discuss the potential climate of particular parts of the world based upon the latitude, the proximity to oceans and the prevailing winds. Describe the climate in terms of temperature variation, likelihood of precipitation and wind direction. Check by reference to the average weather conditions of a town or city in the particular areas examined (use an encyclopaedia or gazetteer – either a book or CD-ROM version, such as *Encarta*).

Concept 4: Weathering and erosion

There are two different forms of **weathering**: physical and chemical. The physical form is caused by the abrasive force of moving air and water or the heating and cooling effect of the Sun. Chemical weathering is the result of rocks being dissolved by rainfall containing various acidic chemicals, such as carbon dioxide from the atmosphere. The act of carrying the weathered material away is **erosion**.

Expansion and contraction

In hot desert regions, rocks can be reduced to sand by the constant heating and cooling action of the Sun. As the rocks are heated and cooled on a daily basis, they do not expand and contract uniformly. This makes them crack and flake apart into smaller and smaller pieces. In colder, wetter climates the expansion and contraction of water as it freezes and thaws can produce a similar effect. Water permeates into the rock (or even clod of earth) and then freezes, expanding as it does so. This forces the rock (or clod of earth) apart so that when the ice thaws, smaller pieces are the result.

Acid rain

This is far from a new phenomenon of the industrial age. Carbon dioxide in the atmosphere is dissolved into rainwater, which then acts as an acid on certain alkaline rocks and minerals such as calcite (limestone) and feldspar (clay). Atmospheric pollutants have added to the problems by increasing the range of chemicals (such as sulphurs from power station exhausts).

Abrasion

Moving air (wind) or water (rain, or flowing rivers or glaciers) have an abrasive action on the landscape. Vegetation will often reduce the effect of this erosion by holding the soil together or by breaking up the flow. In desert areas small particles picked up and blown by the wind can have a significant impact, sculpting rocks through sand blasting. Although rain can have a similar but lesser effect, it is the action once it has reached the ground that is most dramatic. As water flows downward it will begin to cut channels in softer rocks, forming streams and rivers. Smaller particles of debris will be carried downstream to be deposited elsewhere.

Children need to appreciate that much of the natural landscape around us is shaped by the action of the weather over very long periods of time. Rivers, wind and ice all have an effect that can only be observed in the very long term.

Erosion – the transport of debris resulting from the act of weathering from the original site.
Weathering – the action of the weather on the landscape (particularly rocks).

● The Grand Canyon in the USA was formed as the result of river erosion – it is 350km long and up to 1615m deep.
● The longest cave system, gouged out from the rock by water, is 560km long – and this is only the portion that has been explored so far!
● A stalactite (formed by calcium in water dripping from the ceiling) 59m long has been found in a cave in Spain.

Land is weathered only where there is no vegetation.
It's true that without vegetation the land is more susceptible to erosion, but erosion isn't stopped entirely by vegetation. Where agriculture has resulted in large areas of land being cropped and then ploughed, the loose soil has been more open to being washed or blown away. For this reason a more sustainable approach to arable farming is being employed in many parts of the world. However, in others, such as the Amazon basin, the forest is being cleared for farmland, but the soil is so poor and the rains so dependent upon the forests that the land soon becomes desert. Arable land is unable to retain as much water as can be found in the mass of vegetation in the original forest. The lack of vegetation allows the land to drain much more effectively, leading to the desert conditions forming.

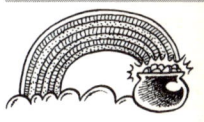

With all of this weathering and erosion, why isn't all the land just flat?
All the time that mountains and hills are being worn down, new ones are being formed as the result of volcanoes and movements in the Earth's crust. It all happens so slowly that one tends to balance out the other in the very long run.

Changing weather

Soil busting (investigating, observation)

As a demonstration, take a clod of wet soil and freeze it. Observe what happens as it defrosts – the clod should break up as the ice expands and then contracts as it thaws.

Sandstorm (observing, exploring)

Please note that goggles should be worn and sand should not be blown towards anyone.

Place a few larger stones on a tray of dry sand. Individual children can gently blow the sand in one direction using a drinking straw. What happens to the sand? Where does it build up? What happens to the sand drifts when the direction of the 'wind' changes?

Careful farming (observing, testing)

Rest a tray of soil, raised at one end, on a large plastic sheet (this can be messy!). Using a watering can, rain water down on to the soil. What happens? Try 'ploughing' furrows using a pencil up and down the slope – compare this to what happens if the furrows are across the slope. To reduce erosion it is best to plough across the slope.

Resources

Weather measuring devices – anemometers (or vent meters), rain gauges, thermometers, barometer (all useful in terms of learning how to read scales)

Remote sensing devices – by connecting these up to the computer it is possible to record several weather factors continuously: temperature, light (an indication of cloud cover), wind speed (via a rotation measure), wind direction (via a movement sensor)

TV/newspaper weather reports – to interrogate and discuss

References

Multimedia CD-ROM encyclopaedia (such as *Encarta*)
Phillips School Atlas
Pocket Guides: Life Processes and Living Things by Neil Burton (Scholastic)
Pocket Guides: Physical Processes by Neil Burton (Scholastic)

Websites

www.bbc.co.uk/weather
www.sutton.lincs.sch.uk/weather/index.htm
www.meto.gov.uk

Materials and their properties
GLOSSARY

Atom – the smallest lump of an element.

Compound – a material made from different atoms chemically blended together in precisely the same proportions throughout.

Covalent bonding – atoms held together through shared electrons.

Electron – a small (in sub-atom sized terms) negatively charged particle.

Element – a material made from only one type of atom.

Giant structure – an arrangement of ions of atoms, held together by attractive charges of positively and negatively charged ions (hence 'ionic' bonding).

Ion – an atom that has either gained or lost an electron to give it a negative or positive charge.

Neutron – a relatively massive (in sub-atom sized terms) neutrally charged particle.

Nucleus – the centre of the atom containing protons and neutrons.

Proton – a relatively massive (in sub-atom sized terms) positively charged particle.

THE NATURE OF STUFF

Artefact – a manufactured product.

Brittle – a material that breaks suddenly when a force is applied to it.

Chipboard – a wood-based product manufactured by compressing wood chips and glue to make solid sheets

Elastic – a material that returns to its original shape following deformation.

Ergonomics – is the study of humans and their interaction with their surroundings, in particular tools and furniture (how else could chairs be made so comfy?!).

Ferromagnetism – a form of magnetism that can lead to magnetism being retained to make a permanent magnet.

Hard – a material that is difficult to scratch or dent.

PROPERTIES OF MATERIALS

Opaque – blocks light.
Photon – a particle of light.
Plastic – a material that does not return to its original shape following deformation.
Polymer – long molecule constructed of a 'chain' of atoms.
Tough – a material that breaks slowly and in parts when a force is applied to it.
Translucent – allows light but not coherent images through.
Transparent – allows images through.

CHANGING STATE

Boiling – the process by which molecules in a liquid change into a vapour (much faster change than evaporation).
Condensing – the change of a vapour into a liquid, giving out energy as it changes.
Evaporation – the process by which molecules on the surface of a liquid change into a vapour.
Freezing – the change of a liquid to a solid, giving out energy as it changes.
Gas – a material that can spread out to fill an enclosed container.
Latent heat – the energy change in a material that leads to a change of state rather than temperature.
Liquid – a material that adopts the shape of the bottom of a container.
Melting point – the point at which a solid substance liquefies.
Solid – a material that retains its shape.
Vapour – the gaseous form of a material more commonly found in a liquid or solid form. A vapour is different from a gas in that a change of state can come about by changes in pressure alone, unaided by changes in temperature.
Viscosity – the resistance to the flow of a liquid.

MIXING AND SEPARATING

Chemical change – one where the molecular structures of the combined substances are broken down and recombined to form new substances, making separation impossible (or nearly so).
Colloid – a suspension of small particles of one substance within another.
Distillation – the collection of an evaporate by cooling.
Filtration – the collection of larger particles in a mixture.
Gel – a particular mixture of solid and liquid that will produce another solid.
Miscible – a mixable mixture (leading to an even distribution of the substance throughout).
Physical change – one where the molecular structures of the combined substances stay separate, allowing separation to take place.
Saturation – point at which no more solute can be dissolved in solvent.
Sedimentation – allowing suspended particles in a mixture to settle.
Solute – the substance that is dissolved.

Solution – the dispersion, at a molecular level, of one substance within another.
Solvent – what the material is dissolved in.
Suspension – a substance that contains small particles of another substance floating around in it.

CHEMICAL CHANGES

Anaerobic – respiration without the use of oxygen.
Catalyst – a substance that speeds up or increases a chemical reaction.
Chemical change – one where the molecular structures of the combined substances are broken down and recombined to make new substances.
Coagulate – bunching together of protein molecules.
Combustion – reaction between a hydrocarbon and oxygen to produce carbon dioxide, water and heat.
Endothermic reaction – one that requires heat to occur.
Exothermic reaction – one that transfers heat to the local environment.
Monomer – a relatively small molecule made from a few atoms.
Physical change – one where the molecular structures of the combined substances stay separate, allowing separation to occur.
Polymer – a long chain of chemically bonded monomers.
Polymerisation – the process of combining monomers to form polymers.
Reactants – substances that react with one another chemically to form a new substance (or substances).

CHANGING EARTH

Core – iron-based central portion of the Earth which is so hot and under so much pressure it acts like both a liquid and a solid.
Earthquake – a release of built up stress caused by the movement of the Earth's crust.
Extrusive – igneous rock formed on the surface of the Earth.
Hydrosphere – the Earth's layer of surface water (mainly oceans and polar ice caps).
Igneous – rocks formed from cooling magma.
Intrusive – igneous rock formed by slow cooling within the Earth.
Lava – magma that has reached the surface.
Lithosphere – surface crust of the Earth, 5 to 50km thick.
Magma – molten rock beneath the Earth's surface.
Mantle – the semi-liquid rock layer between the core and the crust.
Metamorphic – rocks that have been transformed by heat and pressure.
Molten – a solid that has been turned (melted) into a liquid through heating.
Pyroclast – a lump of hot volcanic material.
Sedimentary – a rock formed by particles being deposited in layers.
Seismograph – a meter that measures movements in the Earth.
Subduction – when one tectonic plate is pushed beneath another.
Tectonic plate – a portion of the surface of the Earth which moves relative to other parts of the Earth's surface.

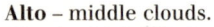
Troposphere – that part of the atmosphere that contains most of our weather.

Volcano – a conical mound formed by the expulsion of volcanic material.

CHANGING WEATHER

Alto – middle clouds.

Cirrus – high clouds.

Climate – the long-term effect of the Sun's light and heat on a particular part of the world.

Cold front – cold air undercutting a mass of warm air (rain storm).

Cumulus – fluffy clouds.

Cyclone – a low air pressure area otherwise known as a depression.

Erosion – the transport of debris from the act of weathering from the original site.

Hurricane or **typhoon** – a severe cyclone.

Isobar – line joining up points of equal atmospheric pressure.

Nimbo/nimbus – rain bearing clouds (darker).

Occluded front – warm air trapped between two masses of cold air (drizzle then heavy rain).

Precipitation – water vapour in the atmosphere returning to liquid form (rain, snow, hail, mist).

Season – a period during the year having a particular climate.

Stratus – layer cloud.

Warm front – warm air rising over a mass of cold air (persistent rain).

Weather front – the border between air masses of different temperatures.

Weathering – the action of the weather on the landscape (particularly rocks).

Materials and their properties
INDEX

POCKET GUIDES: MATERIALS